CW01066534

Beyond Blood

Also from BlackWattle Press

Novels —
Mayakovsky in Bondi — Sasha Soldatow
Shadows on the Dance Floor— Gary Dunne
Wisdom — Rae Desmond Jones (1995)
Short Fiction —
Fruit — Gary Dunne, Editor
Falling For Grace — Roberta Snow & Jill Taylor, Editors
Angel Tails — Tim Herbert
Travelling on Love in a Time of Uncertainty — Gary Dunne, Editor
Poetry —
Flight of Koalas — Margaret Bradstock
The Times of Zenia Gold — Chris Jones
History —
Camping by a Billabong — Robert French
Cartoons —
Living With Adam — Jeff Allan

Send SASE for a catalogue, PO Box 4, Leichhardt NSW 2040

Beyond Blood

writings on the lesbian and gay family

Editors

Louise Wakeling
Margaret Bradstock

BlackWattle Press
Sydney Australia
1995

Some of the articles included here have appeared, in whole or in part, in other publications. Details are included in the author's biography.

Published by BlackWattle Press Pty Ltd
PO Box 4, Leichhardt, NSW Australia 2040
February 1995

Printed by Southwood Press, Marrickville NSW

Some of these stories have been fictionalised, most are based on fact. Names and details may have been changed to preserve anonymity.

ISBN 1 875243 17 8

Contents

LOUISE WAKELING & MARGARET BRADSTOCK

Introduction

During 1994, the Year of the Family, some of the limelight finally began to fall on the lesbian and gay alternative family. The conservative '90s this might be, but in various ways we've been co-opting, broadening and re-defining the word 'family', just as we once did with the word 'gay'. As Susan Harben points out in her 2SER speech, we have as much right to the concept of family as any other group in society. Films (*The Wedding Banquet, The Sum of Us, Priscilla – Queen of the Desert*), TV shows (the ABC's *Kilroy Down Under*, 1994, and *Living in the '90s*), and newspaper articles (*Meet Mum, Mum & the kids*, SMH, 27 Aug. 1994) are finally giving credence to a situation which has been in existence for a long, long time.

Admittedly, media questions about these families are sometimes still a little silly or stereotypical. The opening shot of Miranda Kuijpers and Belinda Vlotman in *Living in the '90s*, for instance, positioned them in bed on a typical morning, whereas other parents weren't given this focus. For the most part, however, the exposure has affirmed the validity of the lesbian family unit. We've certainly come a long way since the sensational tabloid coverage of Pearlie McNeill, her partner Marie and their baby in 1982!

A year ago, during Writers' Week at the Festival of Sydney, Louise Wakeling explored some of these ideas in a paper entitled *Beyond Blood*. The germ of this book goes back much further still, to her earlier article, *Lesbian Madonnas and the Wholly New Family*, (written under the pseudonym of Sarah Vito) in the Lesbian issue of *Gay Information*, 1987. Aware of the almost complete lack of specifically Australian material in this area, (the only other recent publications of note are *Mothers and Others* and *The Lesbian and Gay Parenting Handbook*), the editors always intended to remedy this in a book-length publication. And what better time than now to talk about present and future forms of the family, in this decade of *fin de siecle* nostalgia for the 'pure' family of the past?

The *Gay Information* article dealt with the experiences of a number of lesbian and bisexual mothers, their donors and co-parents. Back then, most lesbian/bisexual mothers wanted greater acceptance of their alternative parenting units, and were pushing for a wider definition of the family. (There have been many changes in the partnerships and relationships since that time, and at least one family unit became embroiled in a prolonged legal battle over access, a situation that shows that in this respect, lesbian families may be no different from hetero-sexual ones.) Whether lesbian and gay parents liked it or not, their new styles of parenting *did* actively threaten the future of the nuclear family. Their very existence made its inconsistencies and drawbacks so obvious.

In this book the debate is carried even further. There is, for example, Lea Crisante's article on the family, its problems and variant forms. She uses the discourse of difference to draw attention to the lack of credibility of lesbian families to date and, by contrast, the flaws in the fabric of the more conventional institution. She notes the success of the most recent version, whereby two lesbians raise the children of one or the other from birth, and the greater viability of this model over the co-parenting of children from an earlier marriage of one of the partners. This is borne out by the accounts of children in this book.

Those who suffered most were the children whose concept of family changed of necessity mid-stream — Cathy Brooker, Pearlie McNeill's two sons, Trystan and Chris, and to some extent Michael Bradstock. They bore the double burden of their own doubts and fears about the situation, and society's homophobic persecution. Lesbian mothers themselves were often the victims of discrimination, sometimes ignited and fuelled by ex-husbands, and for this reason, they weren't always in a position to strengthen their children. Michael, nonetheless, sees clearly the hypocrisies and failures of his friends' seemingly 'normal' families, the sites of drug abuse, self-mutilation and unhappiness.

Dr. Stephanie Bradstock, a few years further down the track, has emerged virtually unscathed. On her own admission 'always an inde-pendent thinker', she was protected by her firmly held ideals, enlightened friends and a degree of invisibility and support during the crucial school years. She is, in fact, very aware of the benefits of having two mothers, and was eloquent on the subject on the *Kilroy Down Under* programme. Dr. Jim Hyde's 18 year old daughter, Alice, spoke on the same programme about the benefits of living in a broad-minded and loving context with her father and his male partner.

The children of the new generation, conceived within a lesbian relationship by alternative insemination — Jay, Maeve, Rowan — don't pine for their families to be 'normal' (they believe they already are) or to change in any way. What they want is for homophobic members of society to accept their family structure. They've understood these things since birth. The parents of another little girl we know are heterosexual, but her biological father is a gay donor. She refers to the latter cheerfully as 'my sperm donut'. It would seem that any family situation is acceptable if it's based on love, commitment and communication.

The opposition point of view gets no house-room here — it receives plenty in mainstream society anyway. Even so, the objections and perspectives of the pro-traditional family lobby surface in many of the contributions in this anthology. What about the hang-ups of straight society, then — for example, that these children of 'deviants' will grow up deviant? We don't think so. They've been burnt too often by an unthinking, even vindictive, society. Then again, they'll probably resist stereotypical gender roles and create the basis for new and different family structures.

The younger children's concerns have centred around their perceived difference at school, and their fears of victimisation for something which to them is a completely normal and happy part of their lives. The other questions thrown up by an angst-ridden straight world — the sexual orientation of these children, the importance of male role-models/fathers — affect each individual differently. In some cases, they have no effect at all, though no doubt much will be written on them in the future. Children's priorities and needs are not those of adults. For our part, we often question what straight families must be doing *right* to create so many people who choose a lesbian or gay lifestyle!

Other children to benefit from this new flexibility in the concept of 'family' will be those with unrelated but committed gay 'uncles' like Uncty Cam. Gary Dunne, one of those donors indispensable to the whole process, explores the humour inherent in vegemite jars. Stephen Dunne (no relation, but a sister under the skin) also exposes the humorous side of donoring. He talks honestly of the pangs and pains of anonymous donoring — knowing that you have offspring somewhere, suspecting they're being moulded as middle-class conservative heterosexuals and hoping there's a little drop of rebellious blood there to save them. Others, like Sasha Soldatow, have metaphysical doubts about donoring, and choose to be retentive about their sperm (at least, in regard to conception).

Valuable information is provided by solicitor, Kerry Sawtell, about the legal rights (and lack thereof) of lesbian parents. Many women feel secure in the fact that they've nominated a partner as legal guardian, but lesbians should be aware that in Australia they can't achieve this in the lifetime of the biological mother, unless the latter relinquishes the right. This is very difficult to obtain in the event of her death. As always, custody represents a battlefield, but fortunately the wishes of the child are paramount once s/he is of an age to be able to express them.

At times separatist, at times more closely allied, more politicised lesbians and gay men find they have never been so united as when it comes to parenting children. This has historical precedents in the marriage of convenience — Vita Sackville-West and Harold Nicolson, for example, married to escape social censure and to engender children. Unusual family set-ups are no longer the prerogative of well-to-do, upper-class eccentrics of indeterminate sexuality. The bad old days are gone, and lesbians and gays no longer have to choose between parenthood and following our natural bent. Lesbian and gay parents are in effect re-writing the script of what it means to live a homosexual existence. However we might infuriate those conservatives who believe this can't, or shouldn't, be happening, the evidence of our success as parents, and the flexibility of our family structures, can't be denied. Today's gay and lesbian parents are ground-breakers.

Postscript: January 1995. The Chief Justice of the Family Court of Australia, Justice Alastair Nicolson, called for homosexual couples and their children to be recognised as a family — under law and by society. He criticised the time wasted during 1994 arguing the definition of what constitutes a family.

SUSAN HARBEN

We Are Family

A speech by the former President of Sydney Gay & Lesbian Mardi Gras at the launch of the 'We Are Family' 2SER radio series, Wednesday 1 March, 1994.

This year the Australian Government has seen fit to announce 1994 as the International Year of the Family. We are just two months into this special year, and already the concept of family has caused much controversy. What an extraordinary thing that a single word, and a word that all of us have some experience of, should press such buttons and cause such controversy and distress.

We are all born of mothers. Most of us have a family of some kind — a Mum and a Dad, sometimes siblings, and sometimes another adult or more who have become our families. Then, of course, there is the extended family construct. Not to mention kinship structures that may not even fit our white Anglo language. But most of us have some experience of family — a family unit, a family support structure. This year, Sydney Gay & Lesbian Mardi Gras decided to use the motto 'We Are Family' on our 1994 Mardi Gras poster.

Because Mardi Gras is a celebration of pride for the gay and lesbian community, we don't usually adopt other themes or mottoes. But the International Year of the Family requires that minority groups, such as the gay and lesbian community, ask how we wish to position ourselves in the discourse that will happen about family this year. What voice will we give? How can we re-contextualise it, so that diversity can be recognised and valued? So that the single model of the nuclear family, which isn't even necessarily dominant any more in this diverse and multicultural country of ours, is challenged or relegated to its rightful place as one legitimate form of family, but certainly not the only viable or healthy option.

Mardi Gras' use of 'We Are Family' has caused much comment — both from inside our own community and from the wider world. It is one thing for the lesbian and gay community itself to debate the usefulness and meaning of 'family' as it applies to us as homosexual people. But it is an entirely different thing that some Australian politicians are asserting that we have no right to include ourselves within the definitional parameters of family. These parameters of course being constructed by the majority culture — them!

Already the gay and lesbian community has been accused of hijacking the term 'family' and of attempting to hijack the political agenda of the International Year of the Family. I am bemused by their use of the term 'hijack'. It assumes that some other group owns the word 'family' exclusively. Well, I've got news for them. Just as no class has exclusive ownership of the concept of dignity; and no culture owns the concept of pride; so also, no group or individual, and in particular not a political party or a paid elected politician, owns the concept of family. Our insistence is one that we be included. We have no wish to exclude any-one else. We just seek recognition and inclusion. One must really ask the question — who's doing the hijacking? And why the need to hold on so tightly to something that's not even in your hands in the first place?

For my own gay and lesbian community — which is a particular cultural group — family is a term that is very much part of our lifestyle. We have, as a group, nurtured the concept of a world family, most often expressed as community. We are a family that spans languages, continents and cultures. Regardless of where we live in the world, we speak a common language; we share a common history; many of our life experiences are in common. Our stories have common threads. We care for our family members and have built effective and often powerful infrastructures to care for them better. This is the gay and lesbian family at the macro level — community — family — a social and cultural construct that nurtures our growth and development and where members are bound by common interest and relationships of care.

And of course at the micro level families are very much part of our gay and lesbian lives. We have biological families — our parents and siblings and blood relations, and some of us have our own children. And of course just like the heterosexual model, many choose a significant other, albeit of the same sex, to share our lives with. Additionally, in our culture, many live with families of choice — one or more adults who become in time and with effort (no different from any other relationship) the social construct that nurtures growth, that shares our life's mile-stones and cares for and supports us.

Nothing very unusual in all of this, really. Very positive in terms of healthy values and contented and supported lifestyles. One must ask why something so ordinary and positive can be so contentious. I think it's clear the problem must rest with the protesters.

Finally, I would like to congratulate 2SER for its vision in having developed this ten-part radio series. Often the media is creating and constructing the news when it wants us to think it's just reporting it. This series is an example of the media truly promoting the discourse around what has become a complex and contentious issue.

What an opportunity we have, in this the International Year of the Family. Our responsibility is to vigorously pursue the reform necessary to make Australia, as a first-world affluent country, a world leader in relevant social policy and legislative reform. Our challenge is to be clear about, and undaunted by, narrow, ignorant and bigoted opposition to achieving this victory.

CAMERON SHARP

When Harry met Uncty Cam

Harry came home yesterday. For the first time. All wrinkled and wrapped in a too-big jumpsuit, he flopped about like thirteen-too-many at the Beresford.

Fiona looked tired. "And I'll probably look worse," which was to be expected. What I didn't expect was the comfort she held in her new role as mother.

Harry lolled in her arms as she negotiated the nappy service buckets and shopping with a free hand. Offering to help, I suddenly found not the shopping but Harry thrust into my arms, as if I knew what to do.

"Just hold his head up with your hand," and I realised the casual voice rested below a new mother's wary eye.

I stood awkwardly in Fi's kitchen as she packed things away around me and Robin from next door arrived with tea tray and biscuits. Fi sank tenderly into the couch, me settling gently next to her for very different reasons. Harry slept on.

Then the hiccupping started, his whole tiny body convulsing, his eyes wincing open and the lips curling as the spittle ran down his flabby little chin. "He's hiccupping!" I said, in a voice normally reserved for choking and cardiac arrest.

Fi nodded, biting into the shortbread. "He'll stop when he wants to."
He did.

By then he was lying along my legs as I sat bolt upright on the comfortable couch, watching his every move, my hand tucked under his back just in case he stopped breathing. I was sure he did every so often, but just as I was about to panic he moved or dribbled. You don't know relief until you see a breathless baby screw its face up and cough.

Huge hands, especially the thumbs. "He's going to be a hitch-hiker," I announced to no one in particular. Fi and Robin smiled. If there's no doting Dad the gay uncle (aunty?) from across the road is the next best thing. If not better. Broken Condom Man is back in England. Not interested. Not his concern. Enuff said.

Harry Best is here and much of the support group is queer.

"Trevor thought it was great," Fi is telling Robin as I half-listen, sip tea and watch the twitches and the expanding rumbling britches of innocent incontinence. "He was great with the gore, when I was throwing up, with the after-birth and everything. The rest of my support group couldn't handle it. It's because he had to cut up bodies for his course."

Goes without saying. Ugh!

"I tell you though, the epidural was bliss. Bliss! I was in another world. The nurse kept saying, 'Wait another half an hour,' but I'd had it. I really hadn't slept for three nights. It was like I had no energy at all ... I was nauseous. He was ready to go but he liked it in there ... so upstairs we went."

The forceps marks are hardly noticeable.

I had visited Fi at King George the morning after. Not in visiting hours. I was happy enough to leave something at the nurse's station but they ushered me in. I guess I do The Nervous New Father Look well.

Fi laughed when I told her. "They call *me* Mrs all the time. I just can't be bothered correcting them." I'm leaning over the crib, Harry a day old, totally amazed.

"He's really ... real, isn't he?" I'm lost for words.

It's a compliment, and Fi grins. "Sure is."

Harry is home. Fi has maternity leave from the refuge where she works. Her co-workers are pleased as punch. The girls can't wait to see Fi and the baby. All around Redfern, Newtown and farther afield phones are abuzz as a family of friends gears into gaga mode.

Not that we haven't had any practice. The baby shower was a coalitionist circus, par excellence, Andrew and Trevor hosting an afternoon of laughter and lesbian lounge lizards.

Nearly eight months pregnant, Fi was wary of the couch. "If I get into that thing I'm here for the duration."

The duration was not as long as we all thought. Knowingly, Fi left work a week earlier than planned. To try and get a holiday before he came.

Harry had different ideas, and three hours after Fi had clocked off from the refuge he was on his way. Personal freedom and individual choice out the window, it's baby time.

Perhaps that's why I have held a distance from babies for so long. I have created a life away from the dysfunctioning het family of my youth. I have control. There is security in order.

Babies give the lie to all that. There's nothing but questions, worries, doubt as to whether I'm doing the right thing, and the endless aching fatigue of need need need.

It all seems about to change. Fi is the closest of my friends to have had a baby and she and Harry live across the road. I think of all the above as I sit on the couch and somewhere through the happy haze comes the sound of chickens clucking. I am being teased but ignore them. I'm in gaga mode.

And not alone. As lesbians and gay men, as 'uncties' and 'auntles', we have shared and are still sharing in Fiona and Harry's lives. In the year of us 'co-opting' The Family, it feels wonderful to know how wrong the bigots are. Being whatever matters not a jot to a Harry, smiling, frowning, and thankfully still breathing as I hand him up to his Mum.

Nappy changing time. This is where the fuzzy edged dream world of ideal baby meets pragmatic pooh management. I brace myself, but by the time I've collected up the cups and said bye byes to Robin the deed is done.

"That was quick." I see Fi smirk. I really must do something about disguising my relief reflex.

There will be other times. Plenty of them. I have offered to help. Uncty Cam. It has a certain ring to it.

LOUISE WAKELING

Beyond Blood: the lesbian and gay family

In the '90s we've heard a lot of hype about family. Politicians and others have bombarded us with a multitude of definitions of the family, many of them backward-looking and reeking with a let's-return-to-a-golden-age nostalgia. You know, all that stuff about how wonderful the Australian family was in the '50s, and how we should be going back to basics. The big problem is, the basics we're meant to return to weren't too hot the first time round. How could warmed-over Ma and Pa Kettle work wonders *now?*

I don't recall too many wonderful aspects of my post-war childhood; my own family's attempt to live a traditional nuclear family life led to mental breakdown, attempted suicide, depression, generational conflict and finally, many years later in 1992, complete marital breakdown. This is a far cry from all those images of happy housewives Handy-Andying the sink and cooking up a storm while their husbands and children wait, knives and forks eagerly poised, for the souffle to rise.

I don't have too many illusions about the good old red-necked fifties family, though I do remember playing happy families with my brother. Our fantasy family comprised the two of us and numerous dolls and teddies who were our silent progeny. No generational conflict *there.* This fantasy sustained us as we watched our parents' relationship deteriorate into mental illness and violence; it allowed us to escape, at least some nights, in our private fantasy jet and ocean-liner. The incestuous undertones of our game, and its pathos, did not occur to me until years later. It is still one of the sadnesses of my life that my real family — the one I live with and its supportive and significant others — is invisible to my blood relatives. The only good thing is that I can write this without much fear of being read by them.

Ever since the advent of the Year of the Family (every bit as tokenistic as the Year of the Child, or any other year), politicians have been making renewed pronouncements about the family. It is as though, by chanting mantras about it, they have been trying to convince themselves that it's still a viable institution. The fact that the family has long been in disarray is not usually part of the rhetoric. When it is acknowledged, as in the address of Federal Opposition spokesman for Education, Chris Miles, to the 1994 media ethics seminar at the University of NSW, 'healthy' marriage-centred values are still proposed as the solution to the ills that beset the family. "The influence of family life is profound," he said, after listing some of its serious problems, such as the 5,000 convictions for the sexual abuse of young children in 1993, and the 500-600% rise in the incidence of sexual abuse of girls in families by males who are not their natural fathers (UNIKEN, 1994).

We've all heard the murmurings of ill-judged nostalgia from neo-conservatives newly arrived in the states of wedded bliss or fatherhood. In 1994, for example, Tim Fischer pronounced that homosexual couples did not constitute a family; rather than advocating alternative relation-ships, the year should be used to strengthen traditional family values. This is neo-tribalism with a vengeance. All I can say is, move over Tim Fischer! It's amusing that those with the most recent credentials are often the most outspoken about the sanctity of the (heterosexual) family, and adamant that no one else is going to get in on the act. On the national and international scene, those who squeak loudest about family values often have appalling relations with their own family members.

What is clear is that 'the looser or more unconventional family groupings' (Hugh Mackay, 1993) are still not part of the official picture. The 92 page report prepared by the National Council for the Inter-national Year of the Family recognises every other type of family grouping but the same-sex couple with children. The alternative family has been firmly put outside the fold, for this family we are talking about is still exclusively heterosexual. Perhaps this is because, as Adele Horin has argued in the *Sydney Morning Herald* (Aug. 27, 1994), official recognition of the 'politically explosive entity' of the homosexual family would eventually involve a number of challenges to many laws which discriminate against same-sex couples, especially those involving super-annuation, insurance, hospital visiting rights and emergency treatment, adoption, authorising coroners' inquests and benefiting from partners' wills in the event of a death intestate.

Tired of their exclusion from mainstream life, gays and lesbians have been following their own tribal instincts. They have been re-grouping in response to the failure of their traditional families to nurture them, and to the attitudes of a homophobic society. 'Community' has become a tremendously important concept in the '90s, partly as a response to

AIDS. A desire for continuity and a stake in the future may have arisen in part as a response to the loss of a generation through AIDS. That desire, for some, may have taken physical shape in the desire for children, for an embracing of one's general human potential as a parent. To the disgust of some middle Australians, lesbians and gays have co-opted the family,

'my real family ... is invisible to my blood relatives.'

and are helping to re-define and broaden it. (Cynics, of course, will suggest that they've been co-opted by it, uncritically letting themselves be sucked into the neo-conservatism of the '90s.)

I am amused by the naivete of those who continue to give unqualified support to traditional concepts of the family. After all, the past two decades have given us every opportunity to ponder the dysfunctional nature of the family structure. This is not to say that there are no happy, functional traditional families. Of course there are. Statistically, most people in Australia still live in some version of the heterosexual family. What they increasingly *don't* live in is the nuclear family with male breadwinner and female homemaker plus two children — the current estimate is that this version constitutes 14% of families.

The job that the family has traditionally been given to perform has become increasingly harder to carry out. This is a situation which in the West has generated armies of 'family therapists', whose task has been to prop up an ailing system inherently out of step with social change. Domestic violence, physical and sexual abuse of children, marital rape, women's double shift and the gender-based division of housework, homeless children — the abuse of power in its many forms — the list of dysfunctions goes on and on, and reams of articles and books have been written on them by family therapists. (Looking at this phenomenon positively, at least it means that one section of the work-force has been able to weather the world recession pretty well.)

Too often, however, family therapists are working with families only at the level of individual change. They take on the task of changing people's behaviour and attitudes — for example, of males to power — without tackling the structures which produce these problems in the first place. They often fail to recognise that the family is a social, political and economic unit, a unit which evolved in response to the needs of an industrial, capitalist society, and is in many respects, no longer equipped — if it ever was — to deliver healthy, well-adjusted and productive citizens and workers. (I am reminded of a poem by Margaret Bradstock in which one of her children ponders the nuclear family: 'What *is* a nuclear family? Is it one that self-destructs?')

Some family therapists now, of course, like Thelma Jean Goodrich and D. A. Leupnitz, have called for a different position to be taken up towards women, men, alternative lifestyles and family. As Goodrich (1991) argues, women who swim against the mainstream by choosing to live with women 'are pushed to precarious depths', yet it is from those 'for whom the prevailing culture does not work that reformers can best learn.' Goodrich has tried to convince therapists that they must stop trying to 'fix up the people so the system works better, and start fixing up the system so the people work better'. More importantly, Leupnitz (1988) shows us that lesbian and gay families are real families, not substitutes for the real thing. They are, she argues, 'contributing to the social fund of information on what children and adults need to grow together and flourish'. For her, 'alternative life-style families speak for human power to say "no" to the most sanctioned social and sexual arrangements, and to resist the policing of their own desires'.

That's why I took the opportunity during the 'Beyond Blood' forum at the 1994 Sydney Writers' Festival to suggest that 'family' should be interpreted as widely and as tolerantly as possible. (After all, the Year of Tolerance follows hard on the heels of the Year of the Family.) Both as individuals and as a nation we need to get beyond the limiting boundaries of blood-relations to something more essential. The Australian nation could be seen as a vast extended family which recognises and respects differences, and accords each individual the right to belong. The family has taken many different forms throughout history and across cultures, and this knowledge can help us to solve the problems of family more humanely.

Alternative families will continue to exist, despite the disapproval and opposition of pyjama-wielding rightists. And what's more they work:

whether they are based on friendship, blended families, sexual preference, Aboriginality, disability, ethnicity, shared trauma or shared outsider status, as with people living with AIDS and their supporters, refugees, prostitutes or the community of dwarfs — or any combination of these. In our re-definition of the family in the '90s, it is the quality of love and support provided by families that we should be focussing on, the quality of nurturing, not the gender of parents, their marital status, sexual orientation or age, or any other perceived 'disability' or difference.

Aboriginal children in tribal situations, for instance, when asked who their mother is, will often point to up to eight 'mothers', making no distinction between them. In the same way, the children in a lesbian partnership often come to appreciate that the grown children of their non-biological parent are, in an important spiritual sense, beyond and above blood ties, their brothers and sisters.

To me, one of the most reprehensible features of the traditional family is the pressure it exerts on its members to conform. Those who rebel, those who are different, are made to feel they don't belong. They are often rejected as a threat to social stability. Pain and suffering are inflicted on same-sex couples and their children for daring to live as though they are a family unit. This pain is something that should not be under-estimated: belonging is something we all have a right to. We need somewhere we can have our identity affirmed, somewhere we can practise being human.

It is quite clear that the '80s and '90s have brought not just greater visibility but also greater acceptance of alternative lifestyles, sexualities and living arrangements. The high visibility and social acceptance of the Gay and Lesbian Mardi Gras has both contributed to and fed off this greater propensity of Australians and overseas visitors to see homosexual lifestyles as legitimate and valid, as well as witty and *chic* expressions of being human.

Not surprisingly, Ang Lee's *The Wedding Banquet,* in which a gay couple arrange a marriage of convenience, and *The Sum of Us,* which must surely represent the screen debut of the lesbian grandmother, have been significant films for a wider audience. Both films impress with their humorous and compassionate inclusiveness. Gay and lesbian literature, too, is beginning to be accepted alongside mainstream literature as a valuable tributary, although it is still regarded as a rather raffish distant cousin whom the fathers, in particular, would rather not invite into the close family circle.

In this more tolerant atmosphere, perhaps, at long last, straight society might learn something from the different ways in which homosexual couples and individuals parent their children. We're at least a long way from the kind of Neanderthal thinking exhibited 11 or so years ago in an article in *Quadrant,* by a woman whose name I have fortunately forgotten. This waspish right-winger argued that homosexual relations were and are meant to be fruitless, sterile, because they gave procreation no special weight. What would she say now that lesbian couples are often proving themselves far more fruitful than many heterosexual couples, 15% of whom are dependent on medical technology to make up for being short-changed by nature?

Lesbian mothers choose and actively want their children, and often their partner's children, and rear them without the physical presence of the father in the home. It should not be assumed, however, that they do so in an atmosphere of hostility towards men. Many of them come from families where there are men — brothers, fathers, in-laws. They have simply chosen to put their partnership with a woman first.

The very idea of sexuality and family structure as something you *choose* is horribly threatening to conservatives in our society, of course, who see both as God-ordained, immutably fixed and part of the natural order. By contrast, many heterosexual couples do not prepare themselves for family life, do not choose freely and do not examine their motives or presumed fitness for parenthood, or for life with a partner. They don't consider whether they are being selfish in seeking parenthood. Because it is compulsory and expected as a way of fulfilling themselves as males and females, they presume they will be naturally good at it. Men, in particular, however, continue to see parenting as women's responsibility. Recent surveys have indicated that women still do around 80% of parenting and domestic tasks (Merran White, 1993/4). This means working women are still doing almost a double shift.

Despite the horrified predictions by ultra-rightists that lesbians would bring up deviant and maladjusted children, there is no evidence to suggest that this is happening. Given that more boys seem to be born to lesbian mothers than girls (again, I don't have firm statistics on this), lesbian parents don't seem to cope too badly without a resident male role-model. Maybe, because the odds are stacked against them by society, they try harder, but their children are usually a credit to them, as was obvious on the *Kilroy Down Under* programme filmed at Taronga Park in mid-1994. The subject for debate was the suitability of gay and lesbian, older and single people as adopting parents. It was concluded, perhaps obviously, that children need love. Age, gender, sexual choice or marital status are irrelevant to the capacity of individuals to provide a loving environment for children.

(Some of the other participants, such as the infertile couple desperately wanting to adopt, were angry that a child would be even less attainable for them if adoption was extended to gay couples. They skirted around 'the enemy' as though we were escapees from the zoo next door. Unaware that the two clergymen present were gay, and not their natural allies, they tried to make common cause with one of them after the debate. "Whose side are you on?" they asked, and were forced to retreat in confusion when he expressed sympathy with the idea of gay adoption.)

Perhaps lesbians make good parents because they are accustomed to thinking beyond the gender divide, and because they and their children frequently have ongoing friendships with significant males — whether the grown children of partners, sympathetic gay men, the partners of grown-up children or other members of their families of origin. This to me is a great improvement on the unreconstructed male's attitude of protectiveness towards the 'fruit of his loins', and indifference or even hostility towards the fruit of anyone else's.

The children of such families also have access to lesbian and gay friends who are happy to play 'aunty' and 'uncle' to them and who, though they have wisely arranged their lives not to include rearing children, still find time spent with other people's children valuable and pleasurable. They do it on their terms, and you learn not to ask for more; after all, they chose not to be involved in the messy, manic side of close feral parenting. The best thing, of course, for a support person, is being able to hand them back! (Not all lesbians are so supportive, however — I remember the time a well-meaning friend offered her big dog as sole babysitter for our small children, and seemed quite puzzled that we didn't leap at the opportunity!)

Some lucky lesbian mothers also have access to grandparents for emotional support as well, although this situation varies from family to family. Some grandparents are so busy with their own mental, physical and marital breakdowns that they fail to involve themselves at all, being well on the way to becoming children again themselves. With them, you are lucky to get a telephone call asking how the children are. In some cases, the best that can be hoped for is an uneasy *de facto* arrangement of partial acceptance — as long as nothing is actually discussed.

Emotional support, material assistance, and cultural identity are often denied to alternative families unless they have very enlightened families of origin. On the other hand, aged parents often make demands on lesbian daughters which create extra burdens on *their* families. The assumption is made that because there is no husband taking your energies, there is no one. The partner is conveniently invisible, even if the children are not. This means you are free to attend motor registries with aged parents or haggle for an hour over the price and merits of a baby fridge. Siblings, too, can be a source of pain in their blinkered denial of the validity of a long-term relationship, while they themselves stagger through one version after another of 'And then I met another woman/man'.

I suggest we cast off the puritan blinkers and recognise that family, whoever they are and however 'beyond blood', can and often do help to make our existence just a little more bearable. A non-kinship family is quite often a family away from family, the one that individuals have recourse to when their own 'blood' won't have a bar of them and their difference. Nothing is likely to be achieved by romanticising the traditional family, or by defining it so narrowly it sounds like the sort of private club where most of us wouldn't be allowed past the door. It is equally dangerous to romanticise the alternative family, and imagine that *any* family unit is perfect. (During one of the usual domestic dramas this week, my eldest son expressed the view that 'this family sux'. In other words, he might not think we're perfect, but he never doubts for a minute that we're a family!)

Our society needs to free up its thinking and be willing to explore new paths, new ideas, new forms of being a family. In any case, even traditional families have to transcend blood-attachment as a basis for relating to each other — the very title of the 'Beyond Blood' session which this contribution grew out of assumes that families are united by blood, yet husbands and wives, in mainstream Australian culture at least, are not usually related. They are often strangers, and from different sides of the gender-divide, yet are seen as forming a natural unit through producing children. That's the theory, in any case.

In those ethnic groups which, for property reasons and preference for close-knit extended families, countenance close relatives marrying, custom overrides education and current medical knowledge. The problem is that 'keeping it in the family' can mean that the children of such unions will suffer avoidable congenital diseases or be physically or mentally retarded, a fact to which many teachers can attest. So much for blood.

It's important to look more closely at lesbian and gay families in our society because they are raising children differently, sometimes at first hand and on the front line, and sometimes from a reserve position. I don't know how many lesbian and gay families there are — a recent survey commissioned by *Lesbians On The Loose* found that a third of lesbians either were already mothers or planned to become parents in the next few years — but the fact is, they're out there, bringing up children against the odds. As we've seen, they can't necessarily count on emotional and/or financial support from their families of origin, and they are rarely accorded the kind of acceptance that would make their task of rearing children easier. Their relationships are not recognised by the state — and some probably would not want them to be, since this would bring unwelcome invasion of privacy. (Although this situation might change with the next census, in which same-sex couples will be recognised for the first time in this country.)

Neither school nor neighbourhood networks provide support, either, unless they are lucky to live near other alternative families, or unless they choose to remain closeted. Even then, their children are challenged in the playground (often by children with no fathers) to account for having two mothers. They are frequently questioned by these other children, feeding off the curiosity of parents, no doubt, as to their mothers' sexuality. Children can be cruel, once they detect a reason for victimising another child. Discrimination, name-calling and harassment are par for the course in the school-yard. Even here, you've got to laugh, for the name-calling is sometimes a little misinformed; some kids at our local school, for instance, think that a poofter is someone who farts a lot.

Some children of lesbian parents have to cope with homophobia from teachers as well, not only in the average suburban primary school, but also in supposedly trendy inner-city schools, selective and private schools, where difference is soon sniffed out and punished. These situations often cause pain to lesbian mothers and their children. They must either embrace an attitude of embattled 'outness' (in more ways than one) or keep silent 'for the sake of the children'.

On the positive side, non-parturitive partners and friends are just as vital in a long-term stable homosexual family as any husband and father who is accorded status merely by virtue of 'blood'. I wouldn't hesitate to say that partners are far more involved than the traditional husband, even the New Age variety, in the day-to-day grind of nappy-washing, homework hassles and drown-proofing children at the local swimming pool.

There is no gender division of labour between lesbian parents, and power is more equally shared than it is between men and women in the traditional family. Children, therefore, do not pick up a hidden agenda about sex-role stereotypes that will reproduce itself in their own personal relations later. They relate to both partners as friends and mothers, as essential people in their lives. Those partners who have been there since the birth are so deeply intertwined, often, that the children's behaviour is just as likely to be a reflection of the beyond-blood partner as it is of the biological mother, giving rise to the frequent and ironic comment: "He takes after you!"

You only have to listen to small children use the word 'mummy' to refer to either partner in a long-term relationship to understand that it refers, more than anything, to a nurturing person who is there for them, who bolsters their self-esteem when the world batters it, who provides assurance in the face of society's hard-bitten refusal to tolerate difference, who teaches them how to be a human being in a world divided against itself. The local pre-school registered disapproval when they heard my youngest son call both of us 'mummy' (an intervention which they should not have made, since I don't believe I have a monopoly on the term). He quickly dropped it. In the past few months he has opted to skirt that minefield by calling us both by our first names instead — thus causing another hiccup!

To me, finally, 'family' is any group of nurturing — preferably mutually nurturing — individuals whose interactions help to sustain their existence. Blood is not important, good parenting and good nurturing are. There are no magic formulae for this; same-sex couples with children are in the same boat as all parents — you muddle through, you do what you can according to your lights, you make mistakes. Before the Fred Nile-ist bananas in pyjamas leap to their feet to howl me down, I'd just like to say that I believe people have a choice in what kind of family they want to belong to. Straight society, of course, sees no other path but what Adrienne Rich once called 'compulsory heterosexuality'.

This majority has always been in a position to define reality for everyone else. That is probably why the misguided concept that homosexual families are deviant and will create deviant children still has potency in our society in the '90s — particularly for those to whom heterosexuality is still a biblical imperative. I don't want to waste time on such negative stereotypes as the hysterical Right promotes about lesbians and gay men generally. I tend to agree with Edmund White, who in a speech given at the Centre for Lesbian and Gay Studies in New York said that 'gay children do not usually grow up in gay families.'

What kind of children do grow up in gay and lesbian families, I wonder? I don't know if many of them will be gay or lesbian — living in the context of a homophobic society is quite effective enough as aversion therapy. Rebellion against their parents' choices is probably inevitable. Given that their fathers are chosen with certain optimum qualities in mind, however — intelligence, creativity, political awareness, skin colour and looks — and that their mothers are writers, doctors, chemists, teachers, artists or sociologists, I suspect they are going to be wonderful, talented, broad-minded and tolerant people, just the sort of citizens Australia can do with as it moves into the 21st century.

Goodrich, Thelma Jean, 'Women, Power, and Family Therapy: What's Wrong with This Picture?', in *Journal of Feminist Family Therapy,* Vol. 3 (1/2) 1991, p. 30, 33.

Horin, Adele, 'Meet Mum, Mum and the kids', *SMH,* August 27, 1994.

Leupnitz, D.A., *The Family Interpreted: Family Theory in Clinical Practice.* N.Y. Basic Books Inc., 1988.

Mackay, Hugh, *Reinventing Australia: the mind and mood of Australia in the '90s.* Pymble, A & R, 1993.

'Families not dying — just need support', *UNIKEN,* 7 October, 1994, p. 10.

White, Merran, 'The future of relationships', *21C,* Summer 1993/4, p. 97.

SUE OGLE & ANNIE HOLSTOCK

More than a gift

'Our sons must become men — such men as we hope our daughters, born and unborn, will be pleased to live among.'   Audre Lord, Sister Outsider

I had always wanted a child. At about the age of seven I began to dream of the perfect family I would create. We would all walk around in the nude, touching, laughing and crying. Passion would not be confined to 'cross words' and would be much more than the day my father threw a plate full of food at the back windows. This highlight, albeit a scary highlight, of my childhood, was an act my mother never forgave.

After the amniocentesis we made a special trip to see my parents. I told my father I was pregnant and he wanted to know who the father was and whether he would support me, 'support' in the old-fashioned sense of the word — ie pay. Not unreasonable as he has supported his wife whom he did not want to work and who has never had a bank account, his daughters, grand-daughter, parents, parents-in-law and our Aunty Muriel, not a blood relative, but the longest living of four sisters. Muriel, Ivy, Em and Mabel provided my mother with the support she needed when we were babies, her blood relatives not being available owing to distance, geographic and emotional.

I'm a coward. I made Annie tell my mother. My mother said, "She's not even good with children. She'll be a laughing stock. She'll lose her job."

Later, when we had a cup of tea and discussed the weather, the news and the disasters occurring all over the world, she glowered at me and spat out, "Don't expect me to be happy ..."

Happy! She was furious. Seething with white hot rage. My father rang and begged for help with her. I couldn't do it this time. I had conceived by GIFT, months of blood tests, ultrasounds and five laparo–scopies whilst working full time. I had anguished over the decision to have a child who would not know his father. A breeze compared to the stress my mother wanted to subject me to. A mis-carriage, no thank you. Dad, I thought, you're on your own. He sent her to America to stay with my sister, daughter number two.

A fury. A spitting fury. My mother. The woman who loves fine bone china, antique furniture, subscription concerts and Mass on Sundays. Furious, supposedly because I had defiled God with my disgusting acts. The real problem came to light when we saw my father whilst she was away. He muttered, "Who is your obstetrician? Dr. Begg looked after your mother. I remember when they rang to tell us the baby was dead."

Their first born. A son, who was 'the spitting image of his father'. I asked her much later what she felt when the baby died. "Nothing much. I didn't know him very well, he was only a week old."

My mother, I think you can see, drops great one-liners. I can laugh about it now. Then I wanted mothering, longed for it. We were lucky. Friends, alternative mothers, rushed to fill the gap. One friend, Val, was special. She loved and cherished the three of us and sang to him. Rejoiced.

The priest came too late to baptise my dead brother. His soul remains in limbo and can never go to heaven! The funeral, if there had been one, would have been in black, not white, as is usual for a child. Instead, they slipped the baby down the chute with the swabs and syringes. My father left the Church and joined the Masons. My mother had another baby twelve months later. Me. I wasn't him, but they still stuck a cricket bat in my hands at two. Part of me is very glad they did. My mother, however, brought out the photo recently, commenting, "You were butch even then."

Butch! What a word for my mother to use. The depth of her fury, her grief, her lasting sorrow.

I can't help you any more, Mum. I am a mother now and look forward as well as back. I thought a boy in our family might heal us all but he has opened up old wounds for you. I am whole. He is loved and happy. Our family, my family, is full of passion and love and nudity. He can hit me and I can hold him; Annie and I can rage and make up. When he laughs people turn their heads — it's a deep, gravelly belly laugh. They are surprised to see a small blond chunky boy. He's a boy full of fun and joy, who's good at crying too.

A formal baptism — we went through it for my mother's sake. That is, after I found a school friend to agree to baptise him. No other priest would. But the real celebration came at four months with a pilgrimage to Aotearoa, my home of ten years. My other family, those who know and love me, brought food and gifts and words. This family is not tied to me by blood, but feel like sisters, mothers, brothers and fathers. Close. Proud of me.

We tramped past the pole house, heading west towards the sea, to a place not far from where *The Piano* was filmed. Muriwai, a wild place, my place, a place I want my son to know.

The day was sunny and mild. Perfect for the climb. Ben was in the front-pack. Secure. Down below was the black beach and pounding surf.

'the real celebration came at four months with a pilgrimage to Aotearoa'

I grabbed the rope with both hands and abseiled to the beginning of the flax path. The others snaked down slowly after me. An hour it took, to descend, traverse the rock platform and reach the beach. The rock wall behind us formed a huge amphitheatre echoing the sound of the sea and the wind.

We made a circle and I spoke first, reading from *The Prophet:* "Our children are not our children ..." Then I wished Ben a love of the sea like mine and my father's, his grandfather's love of the sea. Someone had a red and yellow golf umbrella. Bronwyn shaded each person as they held Ben in turn and spoke to him, offering him insights and spiritual gifts — a love of the forest, a happy childhood, self-esteem, a sense of humour. Stripped naked, we carried him to the sea and poured water on his head: then we swam like dolphins, thrashing and laughing. Ecstatic. After-wards we built a big fire and ate together. He was still on the breast. Ben's Naming Ceremony is recorded in a special album — words and pictures. Looking at it now, I see myself feeding him back on top of the cliff.

Breast feeding. I loved it. I felt I had moved into my body. Finally. Before, I had enjoyed being fit, thin, strong, and now other more feminine aspects of my body and nature were fulfilled. At medical school they told us that some women preferred not to breast feed because it was too erotic. After that I was desperate to suckle a child. It is erotic. Many things about babies and small children are erotic, I think. Their smell of milk, of stale urine, their perfect miniature bodies and silky skin. They're made that way to be loved and squished. A friend, with whom I trained, a mother of eight, told me that the more love you put in at this end the more they will have stored up to give out later in life.

Spoilt. He's spoilt. Don't spoil him. Everyone else is concerned about this, even the baby health nurses who use this word about children under twelve months. It's certainly in the texts — most of which are written by men. Men, what would they know about being a mother, or even a full time carer. Two mothers. He'll be spoilt rotten. A sissy. He won't be a real man. Boys don't cry — it's a quote. Yes, I heard my mother saying it to him.

Now I work and Annie cares for him in the daytime. When I come home I say, "Ben, tell me about your day."

This is the best time of my day. If ever I'm distracted, he says, "Mum, about my day."

He can talk almost properly now and he tells me about the big trucks and tractors and caterpillar D4s he has seen. He reads letters and numbers too, but only if they are written on trucks on their number plates. Some things are biological (his maleness) and others (his sense of humour, very like Annie's) are beyond blood.

Annie's Story

The fortune teller at the Poorman's Market in Hong Kong held my hand. It would be better in Mandarin he said. But the messages were still clear:

1. You will have a son
2. You will be rich
3. You will be famous
4. You will die at eighty-one — it will take a week and not much pain
5. Your mother talks a lot and is very strong but your father does love you.

As I was thirty-seven, unmarried and in love with a woman, I dismissed the idea I would have a son, along with the rich and famous promises. I was wrong. Ben was born in November, 1990.

When he was pulled out of Susan, I saw the most beautiful mouth in the world. I loved him from that moment with a fierce passion. He is the only person in the world I would die for.

Susie always knew she wanted a child. When I first met her, her life was totally organised towards achieving that overwhelming desire. I was the great denier. I adored being an aunty and loved my niece and nephew passionately. I cuddled other people's babies, played games with their toddlers, talked to their teenagers, but still said I didn't want a child. I had unknowingly accepted the place my family had for me — the spinster aunty, free to look after everyone else in the family. Encouraged to have affairs, but no commitment that would take me away. Loving Susie changed all that. I realised it was time to grow up and have a family of my own.

Because I left my family for a woman, they have felt justified in punishing me by not allowing me to be an aunty any more. It has been the worst grief I have experienced. Woman or man, I know they just felt rejected and angry that my main focus in life has changed.

This year I decided I was not prepared to continue to compromise. I decided if my parents were not willing to see Susie and Ben then they would not see me. They chose to become more involved and are very positive about Ben and are beginning to care for him.

The relationship with my sister needs more work. I realise I have always been the adult in the family, the strong one they all relied on. I will have to make the overtures if I am to be an aunty again.

Supporting Susie in her attempts to become pregnant by having sex with two men was really gut-wrenching for me. I lost weight, smoked packets of cigarettes and was caught between having to support Susie in her grief each month when she was not pregnant and fear that, if she was, I wouldn't be able to handle it. Finding the private fertility clinic was the most wonderful solution for us. We were doing this together. This baby was our baby. No man to lay claim to him. No man to make his mark on him. No man to negotiate with for weekend access or involve in decisions. As the non-biological mother, I would have been the one with no biological rights or any other rights. I'm not good with rivalry. This way I don't have to share Ben's parenting with anyone except the woman I love. If Susie should die she has nominated me as Ben's guardian in her will. Until the law changes this is the only legal protection I have. Should Susie and I break up I know Susie will want me involved as Ben's parent. As she works long hours, we've both thought Ben would need to live with me. I hope it never happens and I do think having a child certainly motivates you to work on a relationship — there's too much to lose.

We don't know many lesbian mothers but I suspect our situation is unusual. I stay at home and care for Ben and have done since he was six months old. I was supported by the Social Work Department where I worked in my application to have six months' leave of absence. They extended the time when we realised it was too soon for Ben to go to childcare at twelve months. My senior regarded it as 'parent leave' and the hospital accepted that. We had wonderful support, too, from my social work colleagues at a time when both our families were rejecting.

I love being at home with Ben and I have not returned to work. Being the non-biological mother in the traditional mothering role has given me a great deal of confidence which I may not have had if I was the one working. It sort of balances things out. People ask whether this confuses Ben, but, as he doesn't know about traditional roles, as far as he's concerned his mama is the one who goes to work in the family.

As I am at home with Ben, I am often confronted with making a decision about who I explain our situation to. It involves coming out as a lesbian to people I normally would not consider being intimate with. The assumption is that I am the biological mother and there is a husband/father. I find having to correct people in their assumptions difficult and stressful, especially when I don't have any idea of their prejudices. Sometimes I know it's a one-off contact and I don't bother. Sometimes, though, I haven't corrected the person and now it's difficult to keep up the charade. I still get caught unprepared. Recently I went to a new hairdresser and we talked about my hair being blonde and Ben's hair being blond and she asked what colour hair his father has. Where do I begin? I'm not his biological mother, we don't know what colour hair his father has, we don't know who his father is, his mother has dark hair, I live with her and we're lesbians. Oh God! I just said, "Ah, it's a bit complicated," and changed the subject. I felt awful afterwards about denying who I am and who Ben is. Perhaps eventually I can say, "Well, I am Ben's parent but not his biological mother. Ben was born by IVF so we don't know who his father is." It would be much easier to just lie and say "blond hair too!"

I find the use of the word 'father' in our society very interesting. You do not have to earn the title like you do 'mother'. 'Father' is a term people use equally for the man who anonymously donates sperm and the man who is an active parent who loves, nurtures and teaches his child over many years. Some lesbians we've met feel uncomfortable if there is no identifiable father and have seemed critical. Some lesbian mothers, too have been very keen to tell us about who the father is and how involved he is. It seems paradoxical to me that as lesbians they are trying to recreate the nuclear family, or something as close to the nuclear family as possible.

Ben may want to know his father's identity. We can't tell him exactly. There are no records and he will never know his name but he can dream about his father. He can be blond or dark, tall and skinny or cuddly, he can be a good footy player or bad at maths, he can be whatever Ben wants him to be. We know he was a medical student and we think he was probably blond and blue-eyed and had an infectious laugh like Ben does. Whoever he is, we feel very positive towards this young man who generously gave his sperm. The more Ben develops, probably the more we will know about his father — if Ben is a good singer then maybe his father was a good singer. Not only can Ben decide who his father is — he is also free of the baggage — he is his own person and the three of us have to assume he can be and do anything he wants.

Ben likes people. I think this is partly due to our spending a lot of his first three years outside our garage on the street, Ben playing on his bikes and admiring the passing trucks. Neighbours and joggers would pass and stop and talk to him. Men like council workers, repairmen, would interact with him because he was a boy. They would take him on their trucks, let him help carry stuff, fix his bike, joke, tease and play games with him. There are many male role models for Ben, but we also know that boys learn how to be men from relating to women. My two closest supports are hetero women who love Ben and interact with him differently from the way they interact with their daughters. How to raise your sons to become the men you would like your daughters to live amongst is not just an issue for lesbians, but one for all feminist mothers, and certainly an issue for us. We want Ben to be direct, to be able to talk, to express his emotions, to be comfortable about feeling passion. We want him to be as fulfilled as possible, but not at the expense of women in society. Audre Lorde from *Sister Outsider* has written what we'd like to say:

> ... the best way I can do this is to be who I am and hope he will learn from this not how to be me, which is not possible, but how to be himself. And this means how to move to that voice from within himself, rather than to those raucous, persuasive or threatening voices from outside, pressuring him to be what the world wants him to be.

I guess my dream in the Year of the Family would be that people would not assume 'mum, dad, two kids and a dog' is the way all families are. Some days I feel brave and a pioneer, proud to be different, wanting to promote alternative families. Other days I don't want to be a politician, I just want to relax and have my hair cut.

SUE OGLE

The Night Feed

Waking an instant
Before your grunt
Like some nocturnal animal
Preparing to forage
I stagger to pick you up
A huge shadowy predator
But for my smell.

With head flapping blindly
Your rooting mouth
Urgently locates the breast
And catapults onto my erect nipple
You feed noisily
A bat in a tree
Plundering the fruit.

Your first taste
Of life's opium
Sucks at your brain
Setting your eyes lolling
Embryonic junkies
We two
Taking our four hourly fix.

The rhythmic twitch at my core
Gates all other bodily senses
Shutting out the pain and the
Tiresome daytime advice
The moon painless whispers
Weaning is a long way off.

REV CLIFF CONNORS

Marriages and Baptisms

Metropolitan Community Church of the Good Shepherd, which I pastor, performs gay and lesbian marriages, which we call Holy Unions, and baptises the infants of homosexual couples. Holy Unions naturally far outnumber baptisms and, for some inexplicable reason, lesbian Holy Unions far outnumber gay Holy Unions. While I have performed baptisms for the children of lesbian couples, I have yet to enjoy the same privilege regarding the adopted children of gay couples.

Holy Unions are almost invariably family affairs. Oftentimes one or both of the partners preparing for Holy Union have children from a previous straight marriage. I might add that divorce needs to be secured before I will go ahead with preparations for the Holy Union. Such children range from infants to adults. I get to hear much about them during the pre-Holy Union interviews and often meet them on the day of the ceremony.

Jacqueline and Moira celebrated their Holy Union three years ago. Moira's three boys from a 'mixed marriage' live happily with their mother and her lesbian partner. While we were making final preparations for the ceremony, Moira asked me if her eldest son could 'give her away' at the altar. She explained that her father died years ago and that her mother would be present. So, being a traditionalist at heart, she wanted the 'man of the family' to hand her over to Jacqueline. All three boys participated in the ceremony: the eldest gave her away, the middle son was the 'best man' and her youngest was the rings' bearer. Moira's mother beamed and cried throughout the entire event and had a great time. At the reception she took me aside and thanked me most gratefully for 'the loveliest wedding I've ever seen'.

I often visit Holy Union candidates in their own home in order to get a first-hand impression of how they relate. Jacqueline and Moira's house was just like any suburban western Sydney home — the couple, the kids, the pets, kitchen duties to be done, homework to be attended to, television to be watched. The boys welcomed me in their own adolescent ways: the eldest shook hands manfully, the middle brother grunted 'hi' between handfuls of crisps while watching telly and the youngest was all curiosity about why I, a Christian minister, performed lesbian 'marriages.' I felt perfectly at home.

Jacqueline was as much 'mum' to the boys as Moira was. Moira told me that they seemed to respect Jacqueline more because she was firmer in her dealings with them than she was — "Mum's a softie deep down and they know it. When it comes to personal matters, it's always me they come to. When it comes to technical matters, it's always Jacqueline. She's the handy one in the family and the boys know it."

Moira explained to me that she gained full custody of the children due to her husband's brutality towards her and the boys. Before and after the divorce he visited her and made threatening phone calls to her. When he found out that she was in a relationship with Jacqueline, the phone calls became more abusive and menacing. Finally Moira took out a restraining order on him and has not seen nor heard from him since. Jacqueline explained to me, "It's not that he wanted the boys — he never had any time for them and they hated him. He just wanted Moira to be miserable for the rest of her days like he was miserable. The thought of Moira and her sons being happy and living as a contented family filled him with hate and rage. He tried desperately to destroy what he couldn't have. Thank God he failed."

One of the greatest joys of ministering to the lesbian and gay community is having the honour of baptising the babies born to lesbians in the relationship. Michelle and Jean celebrated their Holy Union two years ago. They shared with me that they planned on having children. The 'best man' at their Holy Union was to be the donor and Michelle was to be artificially inseminated by Jean. It worked after the first attempt and I was asked to baptise the infant. Last year Simon was born and six weeks later he was baptised. Simon's gay father was one of his godparents. Michelle's and Jean's parents, sisters and brothers, grandparents, aunties and uncles, cousins, etc. were present at the christening and took great pride in welcoming little Simon into their extended family. I had seen many of the same family members at Michelle's and Jean's Holy Union. Jean is now pregnant with the same gay donor's child, and so another baptism has been booked.

Jean and Michelle often joke about their ability to take turns in bearing children. "Both of us love kids," said Jean, "and couldn't wait to have our own. In this way both of us get to have our maternal wishes fulfilled. Simon is such a good kid and a real joy to both of us. John (his donor-father) is as proud as punch of him. Every opportunity he gets he comes to visit us, but we know it's really because of Simon." They showed me a photo of John cradling Simon under the shower. Michelle added, "He always wanted to be a father but couldn't bear having sex with a woman, so this is the best arrangement all around. He's a damn good father too."

Ten years ago I joined Patrick and Michael in Holy Union. Patrick had custody of a sixteen-year old son, Paul, from a previous straight marriage. Paul is now straight-married with two children and still on the friendliest of terms with his father and Michael. "Because Michael is not much older than me, I never called him dad," says Paul. "He's more like an older brother to me," he adds, then laughs. "My gay brother, you might say." I asked Paul how he felt about his father's gayness, to which he replied, "So what? Some of the kids at school hassled me about having a 'poofter' father and his young 'poofter' lover, but I figured they didn't know what they were talking about anyway and were probably jealous. They could hardly boast." He grinned a beautiful smile. "Most of their parents were dogs. I met them and thanked God I had dad and Michael. At least we love each other."

I asked Paul how his wife, Debbie, got on with Patrick and Michael. "Great!" he replied. "Sometimes I get a bit annoyed because Deb and Mick hit it off together from the start. They're always telling jokes to each other, drinking beer together and having a good giggle. Dad and I are the more serious members of the family but Deb and Mick are the clowns — always joking, playing games and enjoying themselves." "Do your kids know?" I asked. "About dad and Mick, you mean?" he inquired. "Deb and I decided to tell them as soon as they could under-stand, and there's no problem. They love dad and Mick just like Deb's mum and dad, even though Deb's parents disapprove of dad and Mick. That's their problem. Deb and I are determined that our kids are going to grow up broad-minded — no nasty family secrets, no half-baked truths, no skeletons in the closet, no dad and Mick in the closet for that matter — everything out in the open."

My partner and I are the godparents of my nephew, whose naming ceremony I performed two years ago. My straight brother and his straight wife knew about Stewart and me when we embarked on our relationship in 1980. Their attitude to homosexuality could not be more enlightened nor accepting. Present at the naming ceremony were my parents, my sister-in-law's parents, her married brother and his family, and her sister who was also one of the godparents. Selected friends were also present, resplendent with wailing and curious babies. Stewart and I were the only gays present and were treated normally by everyone else.

Within six months of this happy family gathering, my mother died from lymphoma. I often reflect on her words to me after she had a difference of opinion with her daughter-in-law, words which amazed me with their frankness. "You probably think I'm just making this up because

'... the honour of baptising the babies'

we had that argument. But I mean it when I say that I wish all of my sons were gay like you. I wish they'd married men like Stewart. I love Stewart as a son and you know what? Never once have we swapped hard words. You've made a good choice, son. You've made your old mum very, very happy."

MARGARET BRADSTOCK

Old woman, old woman, who lives in a shoe

When I first met Louise, the last thing in the world I needed was more children. I had three already, and a marriage to get out of without too much disruption to the kids' lives. In those days, divorce would have meant automatic loss of custody for me. All I wanted was a few child-*free* nights and days to explore this new and consuming relationship. Inevitably, though, the kids were our responsibility most of the time, and Louise quickly came to grips with the everyday reality of rearing children. The youngest was five at the time, the others eight and nine, and despite the traumas of breakdown of their heterosexual scenario, and a resultant wariness about rocking too many boats themselves, Louise has been instrumental in their maturation, and is now loved and valued as 'other mother'. Being younger (twenty-four), she shared some activities with them that I didn't, and still enjoys a 'shop till you drop' spree with the eldest. Her range of swear-words was very impressive then, too.

So perhaps it was inevitable that she soon started talking about children of her own. Emerging from the binds of constant child-care into a situation of minimal freedom, knowing just how onerous that care can be in the pre-school years, I was alarmed. Added to this was the comp-lication that at that stage heterosexual copulation was the only known way to get a baby. Both of us had men hanging around hopefully then (waiting for us to hanker after 'the real thing'?), and Louise had one only too keen to oblige in the baby-making stakes. He didn't strike *me* as very prepossessing, but she assured me he already had a child who was 'absolutely beautiful'. More problematic was the fact that he wanted marriage, and would use paternity as a lever. At the very least, he'd have demanded maximum access, and would have been constantly on the doorstep.

So the whole idea was postponed. Once my youngest was in high-school, however, I began to miss the disruption of little feet, began to actually want a baby round the place again, and the main problem was how and where to get it. We thought about fostering, but I also knew I could love Louise's children uncompromisingly. It's easier to rear a child from birth, and not have to do battle with a ready-made social construct. Maybe that's lazy, but I'm very much aware of my limitations.

In 1983 we went on holiday to Bali with the girls, now aged fifteen and nineteen, and the plan was that Louise should have a brief 'affair' with someone cute and come back pregnant. (Yes, the girls were in on the act, and approved.) A lot of time was spent spotting potential fathers, and she finally decided on one who was pursuing her avidly at Sanih Beach. Again, I didn't think he was the handsomest around (would I ever?), but the mixture would probably turn out fine, and she assured me he was very friendly. So, she encouraged him. Unfortunately, by the time he plucked up the courage to come calling, Louise was in the throes of an attack of 'Bali Belly' and nearly threw up in his face as he hovered uncertainly on the doorstep. That was the end of that.

About this time, two of the first DIY babies in Australia had been successfully conceived and born, and we began to consider that option. (It was called AID then — artificial insemination by donor — but with the final recognition of AIDS that name had to be abandoned.) We thought in terms of a pool of donors — invite them all over to a 'come as you are' party — and a diaphragm, which was the way other women had done it. The syringe method hadn't really been tried, to our knowledge. Willing donors were reviewed in our nightly conversations, some of them rejected because of their noses or sun-sensitive skins! (You can afford to be picky when the object is procreation without the ties of love or marriage.) At Louise's thirty-third birthday party we were joking about all this, and suddenly said to Paul, of mixed race and dark skin, "Hey, you're just the right skin colour." "Okay," he replied, "I don't mind."

We finally ended up with Paul and Gary, and another willing donor whom, fortuitously as it turned out, I fought bitterly with over other issues so that his contribution to the scheme was abandoned. Fortuitous because he had AIDS at the time and no one knew, though I think he was beginning to suspect. Some ten months later, he was dead. Had we gone ahead with his donation, Louise would probably be dead now too, not to mention the baby. I regret the quarrel, but maybe it was fated.

Another complication was that Paul was about to marry and conceive a DIY baby with Diane. She urged Louise to wait a few months as she'd be utilising all available sperm for a while. The wedding was a delightful affair, and the Gay Nuns threw a syringe into the circle of guests as they blessed the union. So we began to think about syringes and sterile jars. Syringes were hard to get hold of in large supply — the chemists seemed to suspect Louise of being a drug addict. For some reason we thought we needed a sealed, sterile syringe for each occasion, whereas a bit of boiling water renders a used one quite adequate — after all, the average penis that successfully promotes conception is hardly cleansed so thoroughly! Some of these syringes are still hanging around in the kitchen drawer, eerie reminders of that early time.

Sometimes Louise went to one of the men's houses and I'd run round to the other guy's place for his donation. We were doing it all wrong — freezing the sperm awaiting pickup, and Louise walking out to the car

'My other kids were delighted with their little brother...'

afterwards instead of lying down with her feet up. Sometimes I did the collection and rushed it home to our place, nearly an hour's drive away. On one occasion I dropped in briefly on my older children (two of whom were living with their father at the time). "What's the hurry?" they asked, as I blasted the car horn. "I've got Louise's babies expiring in the esky," I urged. On another occasion, when inseminating, I pressed the plunger too quickly and ended up gagging over a very slippery handful, which then had to be returned to the syringe.

Interestingly, these inseminations worked, but then spontaneously aborted during the first couple of weeks. Obviously, conception had taken place but the result was defective, probably because of our faulty methodology. We'd also tried vinegar douches and early insemination (for girls) but that brought no result. After three or four tries we were becoming disheartened. When a pregnancy test reads positive one day (and very early nausea is being experienced), then negative a week later, it can be very depressing. For the first time in my life I understood what infertile couples must go through.

One night Paul and his boyfriend came round to dinner, and we realised it was about the right time of month for a donation. Without eskies, long drives and vinegar douches, with Louise relaxed and feet up in her own bed, conception was easy. BeBop was on his way. We suspected it would be a boy because of the proximity to ovulation, but by this stage didn't care so long as there was a baby. I took to knitting again, and we spent many hours fantasising about this baby. Likewise, after his birth, much of our time in bed was spent discussing his personality, his looks, his cleverness. (How priorities change!) My other kids were delighted with their little brother, though my older son felt rather displaced and took a while to realise he'd just been asked to move over a bit.

No one could say BeBop was easy! Highly talented and volatile, virtually an only child, dragged through Russia and China with us at three-and-a-half years of age — to the temporary disruption of his world and personality — he's a frustrating, demanding, disturbingly articulate but very rewarding person. We took years to recover from his advent.

Once he was off to school, Louise began to decide the whole experience was so rewarding she'd like to do it again. I was more doubtful. (I have a better memory.) Let me be honest — I love kids, but I hate the ties of fulltime childcare, especially during the infant stage. Once I could pick up a screaming baby and feed it in my sleep. These days I'm insomniac and hormonal, and don't welcome such unplanned intrusions. How-

'dragged through Russia and China with us at three-and-a-half years...'

ever, Louise had her rights too and I couldn't ask her to deny her feelings. "I can't guarantee that I won't walk out, or die," I said. "If you feel you can cope, go ahead. Chances are I'll love the baby, and will do my share. I'm just exhausted at the moment." She went ahead. There was the added incentive that this one might be the daughter she'd always envisaged.

Methodology was much the same, only more informed. Paul would arrive and go upstairs for a 'rest', then come down and play with his son while we went for our 'rest'. ("Why is everyone always tired in this house?" BeBop wanted to know.) We'd agreed that the children should have the same father and that, if he wasn't willing, the whole venture was perhaps too complicated to consider. However he was willing, and could see the rationale behind having the kids equal in as many respects as possible. Again we tried for a girl for several months, with the same result as before. When we went directly for ovulation date there was an immediate conception. I was doing the inseminating again, which to my mind meant that already I'd accepted responsibility.

This time there was to be an ultrasound and amniocentesis, as Louise was turning forty. We'd agreed the foetus should be aborted if it proved defective, though had begun to have doubts about the altruism of aborting a Downes syndrome baby. Many are happy, healthy and teach-able — though of course a great drain on the existing family. Fortunately, no such decisions had to be made. The ultrasound revealed a healthy baby — one covering its genitals with its hands, so we still couldn't tell the sex! The amniocentesis, however, caused a tear and a leak. "Tell her to go to bed and rest," said the doctor when I contacted her. "This happens in a small percentage of cases. There's nothing we can do. If it's started to abort, the abortion can't be stopped." So much for medical intervention. That was a terrible night, during which a healthy and wanted child might have been needlessly lost, and at that point its sex ceased to matter to us at all. The leak stopped, and the report revealed another boy. We grinned ruefully, and I started washing all the little-boy gear and thinking of the advantages of having same-sex siblings.

I'm glad they're both boys. That may sound unfeministic, but it's not. We have the opportunity of bringing up two little feminists — boys who like themselves and like women, and have no need to oppress other people. I'm glad BeBop has a brother for support when the mothers seem ranged against him. The boys love each other passionately (often fight passionately, too), and despite six years difference actually play together and enjoy each other's company. JJ is lovable and funny and smart, and I wouldn't be without him. And I'm still laughing about his version of the pre-school Easter Parade song, 'Little Peter Rabbit's got a penis up his nose'! Yes, there's a lot of talk about penises in our household, about circumcision or not, and some would say we're servicing men again. But they'll be reconstructed men, and lesbian mums are probably the best people to do the job.

On the other hand, it's worked out well for the boys to be aware of their father and their genetic inheritance. (It's useful to discover there's madness on *both* sides of the family, for example!) They have access to Paul whenever the need arises, and enjoy visits, phone-calls, birthdays together. Originally none of us thought this was necessary, and maybe it's just a social construct, but especially at the pre-school stage it became important to each of them to be like all the other kids and have a daddy. JJ, in particular, was always trying to kidnap a stray one! Once, on a long and tiring bus tour, during which JJ had been screaming for his home, his bottle, his bear, his daddy, a young man was obliged to sit next to us. JJ paused for breath and asked in wonderment, "Is *that* my daddy?" (BeBop thinks it's a passing phase — he himself is now too mature for such obsessions, he's informed us.) JJ has on occasion invited Paul to 'come and live in my home', but has adjusted well to the fact that 'you can't have that wish, Little Bear'.

They have regular contact with two adored half-sisters, with my older children and their partners (all admirable role-models, if such were needed), and BeBop has designated his 'wild and wacky brother-in-law' his best friend. At the wedding of my eldest daughter BeBop was a page-boy, I was asked to make a speech, and the round tables were so arranged that all parents, including Louise, had equal status in regard to seating. Such acceptance is an essential factor in the development of a positive self-image, and we feel particularly blessed to have achieved it, among the younger generation of the family, at least.

I couldn't pretend our lifestyle is welcomed by all. We live in the Bible belt, on the edge of the western suburbs, where anything irregular is viewed with suspicion. BeBop is constantly asked by schoolmates, "How come you've got two mums?" but he's learned to respond, "Just lucky, I guess," and to parry more confronting suggestions. The teachers, though, respect our family set-up and ask no questions — Louise and I are both 'BeBop's mum' and are equally entitled to discuss his progress and make decisions. These are difficult years for BeBop, but my older kids support and reassure him, and he knows it's just a matter of time until he has more enlightened peers. "Our friends know all about you," they tell us, "and don't mind. Otherwise they wouldn't be our friends."

From my own point of view, I'm a better parent this time round — less irresponsible, more adequate, more fulfilled in other areas of my life. Okay, I might have been an Associate-Professor if I'd had these years to myself, I might have written more books, led a peaceful existence, gone out more instead of falling exhausted into bed and then getting up at six a.m. for Junior Swimming Squad. But life would have been the poorer. How many fifty-two year olds do you find taking up body-boarding and swimming three km a week to keep ahead of the guys, lighting campfires, bicycling and climbing trees? Not to mention having an excuse to buy knight and pirate Lego — which wasn't around when I was young.

And the latest news is that I (we?) may become a grandmother. Our whole household is filled with delight at the prospect, the addition of yet another member to this extended, beyond-blood family.

The Jesse Tree

You sent your afterbirth home
to nourish a tree.
("It better not
leak on the icecream,"
shouts Jay,
as I place it in the freezer.)

Hospitals donate the placenta
to cosmetic factories,
some cook it into stew
with wine and mushrooms
or touch it to the mother's lips
to convey the magic.
Jesse will have his tree.

In the Abbey of Saint-Denis
a Tree-of-Jesse window
enfolds in stained glass
its multi-foliate prayer:
a shoot shall spring
from the root of Jesse
and a flower out of his root.

In reds and medieval blues
his progeny grip the branches,
securely placed
in clefts of the straight-stemmed tree.
Seven gifts of the Holy Spirit
rest upon him,
and (they say) the flesh
Christ took from his mother.

Here, no Madonna
but an ordinary woman
will plant her foliated gift.

MARGARET BRADSTOCK

And how are the boys?

They're part of the baggage
I took on,
I didn't need them,
they're what I was handed.
I guard them carefully,
unticketed, unlabelled.

"Where's Louise?" asks Jay.
"She's out, remember."
"Well, never mind, you'll do."

He swims & plays tennis,
talks 'fifties slang like me,
echoing my thoughts
("the first lap's a killer
but after that you warm up").

Leaving the other one
at childcare,
looking for all the world
like Yoda in *Star Wars*
with his goblin ears,
the little face cracks up.
It's a trap, he misses me.

This baggage,
thoroughly caught up
in the left-luggage space
around the heart.

LEA CRISANTE

The Discourse of Difference in the International Year of the Family

Family life is pretty inescapable. We don't need an International Year of the Family to remind us we're all part of one, whether ours is based on biological or caring relationships, or a combination of both. What we do need is to question how particular family types have fared this year, from the political, economic and social point of view. I want to look at families, and more particularly those headed by lesbians, in the light of the agenda set by the National Council of International Year of the Family, and to explore how this intersects with their needs and expectations.

The United Nations General Assembly proclaimed the year with the theme 'Family: resources and responsibilities in a changing world'. The year was meant to stimulate local, national and international action to strengthen families as 'the smallest democracy at the heart of society'. Those of us who work in the murky area of family relationships, how-ever, often have difficulty finding any signs of this democracy.

The National Council for IYF, funded by the Federal government, has as its theme 'Supporting the many faces of families'. It focuses on two fundamental principles: 1) recognising the diversity of family life (for example, ethnicity, culture and religion), and 2) promoting *social justice* and *social responsibility*. The heart of the matter is that families are 'generations of caring'.

In its information kit, the NSW Government stated that Australians wanted IYF to be 'more than just celebratory'; it was meant to bring about 'significant family policy reform' leading to improved family services, as well as generate greater harmony and quality of life for all Australian families. What kind of diversity, caring and reform is involved, we might ask?

Possibilities for reform can be seen to lie within the eleven agenda items set by the National Council, such as in the following:

Summary Of Aims Of National Agenda
1. To recognise the diversity of families in Australia in terms of their

*composition, life stage, culture and race, and to celebrate their contribution to
Australia's social and economic welfare and cultural heritage.*

2. *To acknowledge the value of caring and nurturing provided by families, and to
better support the contributions made through unpaid work in household and
communities.*

3. *To strengthen the partnerships between families, governments, education and
community services, business, unions, religious organisations and community
groups.*

4. *To address the circumstances and needs of families in disadvantaged
circumstances.*

5. *To promote policies which recognise and support the choices which families
are making in combining paid work and family care.*

6. *To promote gender equality and explore ways in which men and women can
share more equally in the various responsibilities and pleasures of family life.*

7. *To address the significant problems of family violence and abuse, including
legislative initiatives, education and mediation, and better provision of
economic and social support for all affected by family violence.*

8. *To address the needs of families facing personal crisis, including grief and loss,
troubled relationships, alcohol and drug abuse and natural disasters.*

9. *To recognise the rights of families and of all family members, including
children, young people and the elderly.*

10. *To create a family supportive community.*

11. *To develop a proposal for A Statement of Social Responsibility to Families.*

These aims sound desirable, but why, in 1994, was there a need for
an International Year of the Family? The very act of proclaiming the year
implied a re-positioning and revaluing. In line with the New Right
agenda, the traditional family needs to become more central at the
community and government level. Or is it that alternative families, from
blended and single parent families through to gay and lesbian families,
want more of the action, more space on the political agenda?

Not surprisingly, for much of the year debate has focused on definitions
of the family, with a particular tension between traditional and alternative
families, since these definitions represent discourses of entitlements —
who gets what. As expected, official definitions of the family reflect
patriarchal notions of heterosexuality and associated legalities. The
Australian Bureau of Statistics, for example, blandly defines a family as
two or more persons, one of whom is at least 15 years of age, who are
related by blood, marriage (registered or *de facto*), adoptive or fostering,
and who are usually resident in the same household.

The National Council gives a more extensive definition: 'two parents
with dependent and older children, sole parent families, step-families,

blended families, siblings caring for each other, spouse/partners caring for each other, networks of relatives extending well beyond the household, families caring for elderly members and those grandparents who play a key role in child care, families whose structures and relationships may differ according to race, ethnicity, religious faith and cultural background.' This definition is more interesting for what it does not, rather than for what it does, say. Gay and lesbian families are particularly invisible. In any case, definitions do not account well for the lived experience of families, so that as we move away from the stereotypical mum, dad and the kids, the vision and images of family life become blurred.

Perhaps it's encouraging to see value being placed on diversity. But how much diversity was possible/tolerable in IYF? As Normie Rowe, the Kelloggs man, ex-Vietnam veteran, pop star of the '60s, father of two, said at the national launch in January, 'Let's keep the year for the majority. Let's not let it be taken over by minorities', a statement which was greeted with a cheer from the crowd. Normie is not alone, for his supporters include politicians, religious and other community leaders. In the light of this, IYF appears as a celebration and empowering of the 'traditional' family and its dominant discourse based on heterosexuality, biological connection and nuclear structure. But what discourses of difference were possible within IYF?

Feminist post-modernists have focussed on the way dominant discourses produce and sustain the status of those who have power against the competing discourses of those on the edges of society, such as women, ethnic minorities, old and poor people. These marginalised discourses contest the privileged positions of dominant groups and speak for those who have less control over their lives and who are then regarded as inferior (Hare-Mustin, 1994). The main ways difference has been examined have been in relation to gender, as for example in the French feminists' work on sexual difference (Grosz, 1989). This has also involved considering other kinds of differences such as class, culture, ethnicity, religion and sexual preference as differences within the person. Difference has not been discussed, however, in relation to different family types, even though they exhibit competing differences in regard to these same areas.

One of the dominant discourses in our society is that of the ideal family, in which the family is seen as a natural, inevitable, basic unit of society whose primary aim is to care for children. The 'family' is assumed to have always existed historically or, alternatively, to be the evolutionary outcome of social progress. The ideal family consists of a father as breadwinner, a mother responsible for domestic duties, and children who go back and forth between home and school. Parenting roles carry with them ideal attributes concerning masculinity and femininity, which parents must fulfil.

As Leupnitz (1988) has discussed, however, the family as it has been idealised is a relatively recent historical development. The heterosexual nuclear family-household is an economic unit constructed by the demands of the work place which, in turn, it constructs through sex segregation of paid and unpaid work.

Susan Bastick (1993), NSW State Secretary of the Australian Family Association, reflects this ideal discourse when she says 'Family life is based on marriage ... A family isn't, as some have tried to suggest recently, any group of individuals living together in a state of commitment or bond.' This view implies that the commitment of marriage is somehow superior to that of non-married families. In effect, it denies the experience of many of us: my son's 10 year old school friend who lives with his grandmother after the death of his mother and grandfather, or my lesbian friends who have been together for 20 years and have two sons in this relationship. The family as marriage discourse belittles the care and attachment of this relationship.

All units other than those consisting of a heterosexual couple with their children thus fall into the category of 'not family', and are considered in some way deviant, broken or illegitimate. The former need not be questioned or explained; rather, what does require explanation are all those arrangements that appear to fall short or outside of this definition, and so in some way reflect pathology or dysfunction.

Ideal family life is seen as somehow an antidote to the 'down side' of human relationships — family violence and the sexual abuse of children. Uncommitted, unloving individuals are seen as to blame for these occurrences, not the dysfunctional nature of the family structure in a rapidly-changing society. While there is agreement that the job the family has been given to do this past century has become increasingly harder, this is seen as being caused by the pressure of alternative family forms, notions of choice, a decline in moral values, and a lack of support by governments, rather than a conflict between the ideal and the reality of family life in the '90s. In short, the 'ideal' family discourse is big on 'caring' but opposed to the notion of diversity, which it sees as threatening its very existence.

Moving on to the 'real' family discourse, it is clear that marriage has been declining in popularity for some years. One in three marriages ends in divorce, and those who do marry tend to be older than previously and have fewer or no children. The family is the place where physical and sexual abuse of children often occurs, while as many as one in three married women are subjected to domestic violence. Balancing this, other family types have increased, notably de facto relationships, single-parent and blended families. Gay and lesbian families, or permanent couples who choose not to cohabit, are said to be increasing, but since these relationships do not yet form a part of the family definition used by the ABS, they are not officially measured.

To many feminists, the real family of the '90s is the site of oppression — both in its constraining roles for women, and also in its socialisation of children into gendered roles.

To help families function better, as is the general intention of family therapy and IYF, is to help solidify the structures of oppression. The feminist position, however, is to radically transform the family. One way this can happen is to change gendered relationships as they are presently structured, such as men caring for and developing real involvement with their children and women, and sharing equally in housework and childcare.

Many of the agenda items of IYF seem to hold out a promise for such change, but are little more than a politically correct set of statements, with no commitment to real change. In the section on violence, for instance, there is no reference to the maleness of our society's violence. While there is some de-gendering of terms, such as 'unpaid carers', this still refers to women in relation to the care of children and sick relatives.

For other feminists, the goal is more radical change — social change, family change, individual change — with the intention of transforming social relations and, more importantly, the structures which define men and women's existence. This involves creating new life styles, new forms of the family, and critically examining the notion of marriage and families as popularly lived. As Goodrich (1991) says, marriage (and for that matter, the heterosexual relationship) is the least examined and most honoured linchpin in the entire structure of patriarchy. *People* are searched for failures and flaws, not the institution. She goes on to argue for the possibility of different life-styles for women, and a removal of the negative and marginal connotations of the notion of 'alternative'. She lists the alternatives to the injunction that women must make themselves available to men:

> To choose to live in single bliss, to pair with another woman sexually or non-sexually, to mother alone, to lead a woman-centred life with only intermittent attachments with men ... they are choices for, but also choices against what one is expected to provide in traditional marriage and family. (p. 29)

During an IYF which celebrated diversity and advocated reform, however, there was no real attempt at re-definition, restructuring or even adequately describing what currently exists but is rendered invisible under the alternative umbrella. Homosexual families are perhaps the most invisible, since they were not included in any definitions or promotional hype about IYF — unless it is on page 8 of the 'Heart of the Matter', in the question 'Do we unfairly penalise some types of families for being different?' This pervasive invisibility occurs in a society which passively denies or actively attacks the right of homosexual families to exist.

Lesbian parents are striving to create meaningful family systems which are recognised as having legitimate status. This is a constant struggle since our culture and its institutions are trying to pull lesbian couples and their families apart, by telling them they are not a family at all, or by saying homosexuality is sick, or even by destroying their families/children. Child-rearing is hard enough in our society, but made more so for these families by a non-accepting school, community and extended family context. As lesbian therapists Mencher and Slater note (cited in Markowitz, 1991), 'Internalised homophobia is an ongoing presence in both partners. Whether, when and how to come out is a continuing question and negotiating roles in a same-sex relationship is a persistent challenge'.

As well, lesbian mothers must deal with homophobic societal attitudes and practices as they relate to child custody. Lesbianism has been grounds for loss of custody. Lesbian women who co-parent have few entitlements regarding access or custody of the biological children of their partners. Research on lesbian families has revealed potential problems for their children as a major area of concern. In Hare's (1994) study, 72% of respondents were concerned about the effect of peer prejudice on their child(ren) because of the stigma of living with lesbian parents. Interestingly, these couples identified more strongly with heterosexual families than with childless lesbian couples. In fact, their daily lives closely resembled those of dual career heterosexual households. They struggled in the same way with balancing paid and unpaid work and child rearing.

Hare's research also revealed that the lesbians surveyed were very committed to their family and to being successful parents, although they did not feel accepted as a family by the broader society, and felt 'even less comfortable within the lesbian community'. Co-parenting partners typically assumed some parental responsibilities, more so when children were not conceived in heterosexual relationships, and were significantly attached to these children.

Lesbian families, then, are real families. Like heterosexual couples with children, they are characterised by mutual commitment, property sharing and emotional and physical intimacy. Their commitment to both partnering and parenting may, in fact, be greater. Lesbians who choose to be mothers do so against the norm of compulsory heterosexuality in our society, and thus establish families in a context of individual choice tempered by societal secrecy.

In doing so, lesbian families offer possibilities beyond the traditional family, as reformers from whom the prevailing culture may learn. Their existence is evidence of the fact that non-biological ties are just as powerful and meaningful as biological ones, if not more so. While complexities arise in same-sexed relationships, it would seem that power is potentially more equally shared. As well, children are not likely to acquire conventional gendered power relationships to reproduce in their own personal relationships.

These families see themselves as highly valuing diversity and deeply committed to caring, yet none of the eleven agenda items of IYF recognises that diversity should include families headed by lesbians. Lesbian parents with children can't benefit from changes to income tax arrangements for single income families, since they are not eligible as a married or *de facto* couple. They, too, need places in long-day centres and related institutions, but also consideration of the needs of these children in a homophobic context. Disadvantage experienced by lesbian families in employment, housing or the legal system is not mentioned. The crises faced by such families are also not discussed — violence, issues of coming out, relationship breakdown and its implications for non-biological parents, and the isolation of living in a homophobic society. (Levy, 1992)

It is unlikely that requests for emotional support, material help and a sense of identity for lesbian families will be met by IYF reform, since their relationships are rendered invisible, as are the needs of their children. The efforts of lesbians to form families reflect an impressive juggling act, but IYF has failed to affirm their family status — that of two people, with children, who love each other and are committed to being together. Non-traditional families hunger to hear that 'family' means people who care about each other. It creates a sense of worth and identity for these families which are excluded from mainstream society.

Reading the National agenda through the lens of lesbian family needs is exhausting, since it means reading in what is not there, what has not been seen as worthy of inclusion. Which year was the family meant for? Clearly, the cornerstone of diversity is Anglo-Celtic heterosexuality, preferably within a married or *de facto* relationship. Alternative families remain the other, split off from the mainstream, which only acknowledges heterosexual, biologically-based caring. I wonder how the year would have been if it had been called the International Year for Relationships?

Furthermore, IYF reform implies change from within, with no recognition of experiences of domination and oppression. The dimension of power is effectively denied. Perhaps this arises from a political need for the year to be based on a non-consensual view of families. As Goldner (1988) says, we need to question 'the conceptual transcendence of "The Family" as our unit of description, and with it the epistemological, if not moral, idealisation of the family as some kind of "ultimate unity"' (p. 27).

Given the lack of space for the discourse of alternative families, and the unthinking acceptance of the concept of the 'family', it is important to work towards a view of families which takes into account a much broader frame. Only in this way can strategies be developed to deal with the inevitable tensions and dilemmas of love and power between people living in a patriarchal and New Right-dominated society.

Postscript: The International Year of the Family was formally drawn to a close with the launch in November of the Final Report by the National Council. While reference is made to several submissions received from gay and lesbian lobby groups, none of the final recommendations specifically addresses the concerns of the families represented by these groups.

On the other hand, the New South Wales IVF report makes several recommendations including that same-sex relationships are extended the same entitlements, rights and responsibilities as heterosexual ones, and that support services are made available to assist family cohesion.

Bibliography

Bastick, S. (1993) 'Taking the family for granted.' *The Catholic Weekly,* Dec 29.

Goldner, V. (1988) 'Generation and Gender: Normative and covert hierarchies.' *Family Process,* 27, 17-31.

Goodrich, T. J. (1991) 'Women, Power and Family Therapy: What's wrong with this picture?' *Journal of Feminist Family Therapy,* 3, 5-37.

Grosz, E., (1989) *Sexual Subversions: Three French Feminists.* Sydney, Allen and Unwin.

Hare, J. (1994) 'Concerns and issues faced by families headed by a lesbian couple.' *Families in Society,* Jan. 27-35.

Hare-Mustin, R.T. (1994) 'Discourses in the mirrored room: A Post-modern analysis of therapy.' *Family Process,* 33, 19-35.

Leupnitz, D.A. (1988) *The Family Interpreted: Feminist theory in clinical practice.* New York. Basic Books.

Levy, E. F. (1992) 'Strengthening the coping resources of Lesbian families.' *Families in society,* Jan. 23-31.

Markowitz, L. M. (1991) 'Homosexuality: Are we still in the dark?' *Networker,* Jan/Feb. 27-35.

Markowitz, L. M. (1994) 'When Same-Sex Couples Divorce.' *Networker,* May/June, 31-33.

National Council for the International Year of the Family (1994) *The Heart of the Matter — Families at the Centre of Public Policy.* Canberra, G.P.S.

National Council for the International Year of the Family (1994) 'Creating the Links: Families and social responsibilities.'

NSW IVF Secretariat: Social Policy Directorate (1994) 'Focusing on Families: A report on consultations conducted by the NSW International Year of the Family Advisory Committee.'

MIRANDA KUIJPERS & BELINDA VLOTMAN

Raising Jordan

Miranda Kuijpers (33) and Belinda Vlotman (27) have a little girl, Jordan (6 going on 30). Miranda is the biological mother of Jordan.

I had an appointment (this was some years ago) at a Private Hospital in the Hunter region, making enquiries about the Artificial Insemination Program. Personally I prefer 'alternative' to 'artificial'. I was very nervous, and the thought that this brilliant person might have been able to be of some assistance to me eased the anxiety. He (of course there aren't many female gynaecologists & semenologists) told me about the program and then pointed out the prerequisites for being accepted into the program.

From all the points, one and only one, kept going through my mind. 'Your partner is unable to get you pregnant.' I told him that I would qualify in that regard and said that my girlfriend and I were not successful. "Try as we may, she's not getting me pregnant," I said, half-jokingly. He was totally unimpressed and hastened a quick finale to the long-awaited appointment. "Morally I cannot allow this!" he said.

The disappointment was severe and I was unaware of the many other avenues available to me. The one thing I wanted more than anything else, which is so natural, seemed totally unattainable. It seemed unfair that because of my sexuality so many alternatives were lawfully removed.

Then the oddest question arose for me; 'If I can't have children whilst in a lesbian relationship, then I don't know if I can completely embrace lesbianism'. Of course you can't just walk away from that part of yourself. It seems like centuries later, many dyke dramas passed, and I ended up working with this very gentle and unassuming guy. He knew of my dilemma and cautiously suggested that he was willing to be a donor. Previously, I had approached a number of male friends, but my requests were gently rejected. So the proposal so far was very appealing and an unbelievable relief.

I had finished an early shift and he was still on a later shift. I discovered that I was ovulating. I called him, and told him to get to my place as soon as he finished work. Little did I know that this would be one of the most awkward moments of my life. Previous years of alternative insemination (donated by a student friend) were unsuccessful.

There and then I decided — "Let's do it!" He was shocked. "But I don't want to have an affair," he said. "How can you call this an affair— it's so clinical!" The pressure was on. He could not get it up and I just wanted this whole thing over with. Thinking back to the 30th March in 1987, it was hilarious. I am very grateful to the 'donor', but I would not recommend intercourse as a first option.

My family's reaction ... I guess you can never be totally sure of how your family and friends will react to the news of a new arrival into less than traditional and not exactly accepted circumstances. I had hoped, I wished and sent a number of pressing requests to my Higher power, and ultimately it was just a decision made by me for me. Economically I was independent, with a full-time job, which with the onset of extreme morning sickness and migraines and many days absent was ultimately lost. In hindsight, the relationship I was in at that time was unfortunately not emotionally secure and became very draining. In the light of a relationship breakup and with a dependent infant, problem solving and conflict resolution was not one of my strong points.

Nevertheless, on the 5th of January 1988, after 32 hours of labour, Jordan was born. A feisty, gorgeous little girl. Even though my partner (at the time) was not fully involved in the decision-making to have a child, she soon submerged herself heavily in dirty nappies and playful cooing.

Ultimately our relationship dissolved, which brought a number of issues to the forefront. Was she going to have access? visitation rights? maintenance? Did Jordan need a token role model? etc. I rediscovered my sense of humour and sense of fair play — we worked it all out, mostly. Her involvement was minimal owing to unforeseen circumstances. I felt angry, disillusioned and totally shattered. Only now I realise that this was a much-needed growth experience.

And so time went on ... things changed ... Jordan and I spent many days sunning our bums at the women's pool. I worked afternoon shift to pay the rent and saved to buy a ticket for the occasional party and pay for a reliable baby sitter.

I know it sounds like an old cliche — 'when times are tough you do realise who your friends are'. I'll never forget this. Jordan was teething and had a cold, so she cried. And continued crying for a marathon three days. She slept sporadically and I was near wits' end. I had no immediate family support as they were living overseas at the time. So I called Heather, a true friend, and she stayed over with me. She settled me to sleep and took care of Jordan. I could never begin to express the depth of my heartfelt gratitude.

Seasons passed and then Belinda, the woman I had been friends with for two years, became my very 'significant other'. Jordan at two-and-a-half was high on mobility but low on reasoning. She was insanely jealous. Belinda had incredible staying power. Ninety centimetres of constant aggression was all too much for the two of us, especially Belinda. To say that we had an unsettled period in the first stage of our relationship would be a definite understatement. It was impossible, like a war zone. I think I must have held my breath and hung in there for about a year. We didn't give up because we had a commitment and so much love for each other. I wish there could have been more resources available to us in terms of support and guidance for our circumstances as lesbian parents.

I'm not sure if this is a universal experience as a lesbian parent, but it's strange how you have this driving urge to perform twice as well in order to be accepted on the same grounds as heterosexual parents. It's as though you are constantly being assessed. There's a constant over-compensation.

Maybe it's paranoia, but in the back of my mind I was always evaluating and assessing Jordan's behaviour and reactions. Now Jordan is getting older, the obsessive need to be the perfect parent has lessened dramatically. The more opportunity I have to network with other lesbian parents, the more I am becoming aware of how 'ordinary' her stages of development are, and that they have nothing to do with my lesbianism. It is imperative that we construct studies within our own community and research 'what is' relevant and applicable and 'what is not'. Recently I have had the opportunity to read a couple of books which have been quite helpful; however, they were from the US.

Raising children is complex, anyway, and you don't need a degree to work that out; however, there are so many issues and situations that we endure unnecessarily. I suppose that in a sense we are learning and growing, although the lack of networks and written material to assist with guidance creates unnecessary hurdles (for instance, *Toddler Taming within the Lesbian and Gay Community* would be one of many anticipated titles).

Jordan is getting older and so are her friends. Generally her friends are open-minded and open-hearted, like most children. It's their parents' intolerance and ignorant judgmental remarks that the children pick up on. Children do make comments sometimes that Jordan takes offence at;

however, she handles delicate situations with such finesse now. Many questions have been asked about her 'father's' whereabouts and involvement. She simply replies that he lives far away with his own family and that she was a gift of love from Mother Nature.

Ultimately, even though most people have made negative comments, the decision to maintain non-parental involvement with the donor was the most suitable option for me. I won't deny, however, that we have had some difficult moments which sparked off guilt-ridden insecurities: 'maybe she does need parental involvement with the donor'. After talking to parenting friends and experts, I believe Jordan's needs were not being compromised, as she associates with a number of wonderful men. Philippe, my sister's husband, has been a very positive influence in Jordan's life. Both my family and Belinda's family have been very supportive and affirming.

This is one of the main issues: the donor. If you don't participate through a fertility clinic, finding a donor is not an easy task. I found that after the initial discussion with the donor we spoke at length about medical/psychological history. He had a clean bill of health, which is a major concern that Belinda and I recently faced as we are trying for our second child. We scouted around for a potential donor, which was very awkward and mostly disappointing. Finally we found a suitable donor who was healthy and had no congenital hiccups.

Besides the medical and psychological history, another consideration was donor involvement. Even though I had made an agreement (a verbal promise) with the first donor that we would have no involvement and not register his name on the birth certificate, these arrangements were made for personal reasons and owing to the donor's responsibility to his family. To date I have been fortunate enough not to encounter any awkwardness.

A few months ago we agreed to the ABC Television/Documentary crew spending a day with us, filming and interviewing. I realise that more often than not, interviewers have to play devil's advocate, but I'm still perplexed at the absurdity of some of the questions, like 'How will your relationship affect Jordan's sexuality?' 'How would you feel if she married a man?' The questions went on, some even more absurd; however, most were laying the foundations for redefining the family.

When we were asked what a family means, we went on to say that we shouldn't have to define it as such, but we should concentrate more on what 'it' provides and what 'it' should provide. With this type of interpretation there are no specific gender roles and consequently the structure of this unit is not limited to gender role-play; nor would it limit the number of role-players. Thus it would leave room for alternative structures and extended families. Enquiries were also made about how we felt the Rev. Fred Nile might view our set-up; our answer was an obvious one. Finally, 'Would you consider yourself to be a family?' Needless to say, we answered, 'Of course!!' We chose to be with each other and there is a lot of love.

We have a dependent child and we have joint responsibility as caretakers; we provide a safe, loving, supportive environment for one another. We treat Jordan and her needs with respect, and in turn our example and our treatment of her provide her with the necessary ingredients to be a well-rounded person.

No matter how you define or evaluate this framework — we are a family and we need to be recognised as such.

We have, after much effort, endeavoured to set up a support network — a Lesbian/Gay Parents' Group. At present, mostly lesbian parents (and prospective lesbian parents) are involved, and we expect a number of gay fathers to be joining in the near future. The group is in its early stages and, after pushing shit uphill, I have finally found a venue which we have access to. The administrators of the venue are very supportive of our cause and the premises are suitable and cater for our children. Our plans on the horizon are to be partially involved with the Gay and Lesbian Rights Lobby, and to organise children-friendly events within our community.

BELINDA

I came into the relationship when Jordan was two-and-a-half years old. The first six months were somewhat of a novelty. Then it must have dawned on Jordan that I wasn't only visiting, and reality set in. She knew that I loved Miranda, and that sparked serious competition for Miranda's affection and attention. She did not understand that my love for Miranda was different from her love as a child. She was under the impression that Miranda had abandoned her for my love.

This caused tremendous tension between Jordan and me and generally in the household. Jordan became extremely negative, in particular towards me. She became an expert in negative attention-seeking activities. It was a tough time for me because I did not understand and did not have a clue as to where to begin to deal with a situation as complex as the one that I was facing. Also I did not know my place in the household as a parent, because Jordan was not allowing me to get close and form that bond which plays such an integral part between child and parent.

I was not aware of any parental skills to assist me in this matter and felt quite helpless. I was going through a very tough time. At times I felt rejected and also not welcome in my own home. (I really did feel like I was only visiting, and that any second now I had to get ready to go back to my own home.) All I had at the time was patience and a tremendous amount of staying power; I wanted to make this work for all of us. I then realised that there was no written material and no support network for lesbian or gay parents (non-biological parents in particular). Our generation of lesbian and gay parents are now somewhat pioneering in terms of trying to gain visibility and wanting recognition.

It took a good twelve months or more before the tension subsided to a livable, bearable state, to allow bonding and also for me to learn to love Jordan as my daughter. I also had to deal with wanting attention from Miranda when she was attending to Jordan.

Everything was slowly starting to fall into place, until one day when Jordan returned home from pre-school. She was suddenly extremely aggressive towards me and after many lengthy talks with her we eventually discovered that one of the pupils at her pre-school was saying that she had two 'mummies'. Jordan did not take to this at all; she only perceived Miranda as her Mum, and she wanted me in her life as a parent but definitely not as Mum.

Another event which still makes me giggle was when we were in a shopping centre one day. When Jordan saw me approaching she shouted at the top of her voice, "Daddy!" Both Miranda and I looked at each other and laughed (everyone else around us looked on, perplexed). It was then that we realised that Jordan was ready to accept me as her parent, and what she needed was to call me something that she could hold as an endearment, a name that she could relate to as her parent but separate from 'Mum'. It was from that moment on that the naming process began.

We asked Jordan what she would like to call me; after numerous attempts she came up with 'Nani.' She loves this name and it has worked wonders in creating a very strong and stable bond between Jordan and me. Jordan has now established that she has two parents (one Mummy and one Nani) not two mummies. Because of this, she knows she can love and relate to us in two very different ways, instead of getting confused as to which mum has which duty.

Jordan has developed into a very loving, highly intelligent girl and has chosen exactly whom to explain her parental situation to. She has only made a certain number of people aware of the fact that she has a Nani and some of her friends at school now refer to me as Jordan's Nani. This has helped tremendously in taking the stress factor away for Jordan about her having a different parental situation from her friends.

I myself don't like to be referred to as Mum, as I feel this confuses our role as parents. I like the title of 'Nani' and it is also very stabilising for Jordan and myself that the second parent role has been established and that Jordan has a tremendous amount of respect for me.

This reduced the competition that existed between Jordan and me for Miranda's attention and affection. Now there are certain things that Jordan likes to come to me about that are separate from what she would see Miranda about.

We share responsibility over Jordan now. I know exactly where I fit in within the household. This is all due, I feel, to the naming process. It takes away the fear and anxiety that the non-biological parent is trying to replace the biological parent. I therefore think that the naming process was very important for us (not necessarily for everyone), because it set up a whole new role for the non-biological parent in a lesbian relationship.

Usually, outside our close circle of friends, my position in relation to our family structure is questioned and invalidated by people's ignorant assumptions. In most cases I am referred to just as a friend, or I am questioned as to whether I am the 'real mother' or a flatmate. This constant invalidation can be very demeaning. Miranda and I have laid the foundations in that we are out to Jordan, and mentioned it on her enrolment application at her school. All her teachers are aware of our situation and respect us both as parents. We are out in a way that is not overly confronting, yet still safe for Jordan.

Just because I am a woman involved in a relationship with another woman who has a child, doesn't mean that I want to be labelled 'Mum' and I don't want Jordan to be referred to as having two mummies. I am her parent and I believe that a name should be universally created to assist and re-affirm interaction, and to enhance the position of *non*-biological parents within the family relationship.

ROWAN SAVAGE

Sick of hiding

Rowan Savage is 14 years old

Luchetti's at the wooden desk at the front of the room.

"OK guys, the fourteen A's are playing at Newington this Saturday; we'd like a big turn out — choir practice seven tomorrow morning." Great. Seven is such a *little* number. Stuff it. "Oh and … Martin." He takes a sheet of paper from the file. "Dear Ms Wilde and Ms Marsfield, your son Martin Wilde was away on Tuesday the third. Please supply an explanation. Thank you, J. Dillon." I fold the note and stick it in my shirt pocket.

The sunshine glares after the darkness of the room. Freeman hurries out and catches up with me. He's a dickhead, harbours every prejudice you can think of, but he's just someone to hang around with (although not too often, if I can help it), or someone to sit on a bench with. I take out the note and read it again. Freeman cranes over my shoulder.

"Who's Ms Maaaaaarsfield?" Fuckwit. I ignore him. "Two mums, test-tube baby!" He yells. "Who's Ms Maaaaaarsfield?" I start to fold the note and put it away again. Then Brendan appears.

"What's that?" He grabs the note off me and skims it. "I've just discovered something shocking," he says. "Ms Wilde and Ms Marsfield." Shit.

"What's so shocking?" pipes up Freeman. "We all knew already." Grabbing the note back, I crumple it up, stuff it in my trouser pocket and trudge off.

I'm sitting in history, talking to Ho. We trade insults over the general buzz of chatter. Maris stands out the front of the room.

"Test-tube baby."

"Freeman's Mum."

"Psycho Beast."

"Pyro."

Suddenly there is a dead silence.

"Two Mums." The words echo round the room. Nothing. Then the room erupts in laughter. I laugh along with them.

Later, Freeman tells me that he saw the teacher take a step backwards, saw a look of something cross his face. He didn't want to be involved, didn't want to have anything to do with it.

Walking across the playground, I hear Steve talking. He's my cousin, by marriage. ("Did you marry him?" Min asks.)

"Oh yeah, his parents are gay. Bloody poofs." In history, Vic sits next to me.

"Are your parents lesbians? Steve reckons they are."

"Sure, whatever ya reckon." At home I talk to Tessa about it. "He probably didn't mean to tell them. I'm sure he wouldn't have meant to. He's not like that." He is.

They always go on about it. I always deny. Looking at my writing, I laugh. 'They', like some fascist regime bent on the discovery of my private life. 'They' the enemy. Why do I deny it? To save hassle. God knows. Imagine what people would say. Jordy knows, at Club, but I asked him not to tell anyone. If someone like Ben knew, I don't want to even think about what would happen. Now a group of year sevens call me TTB. Test-tube baby. I'm not a test-tube baby.

"Lessssssbians." The word rolls off boys' tongues like sugar. But not sweet.

People are so stupid. They don't realise what's in front of their own eyes. You don't need to think of excuses, they make up their own for you. Guy says, "Jon's so slack, saying that about your parents. Ms Marsfield's probably your aunt, right?" I agree. It's so easy, you don't even have to try. But then again, sometimes you do.

At rollcall, Luchetti hears Daniel talking about poofs. He tells us there's nothing wrong with 'homosexuals'. He pronounces it Hom, not Home. Someone shouts, "Mr Allan reckons you're a homosexual."

"Oh he does, does he? That's just 'cos he doesn't have a girlfriend." Fucking hypocrite.

I used to go along with gay jokes, make jokes myself, laugh along with the crowd. Not any more. I'm proud. "Gay pride!" (Read cynical.) I'm against 'fag' insults. When people ask me if I'm gay I tell them I'm not sure yet. I copped a lot for that.

I tell my friend Gary. He promises not to tell anyone. He tells the first person he talks to. Then he uses his knowledge as blackmail. If he gets angry with me, he'll tell someone. I don't care. Gary tells Mahesh, who constantly teases me about 'two for the price of one' and 'takes after his parents'. I don't deny it. He pussy-foots around, trying to get my back up.

"Two … sisters. Two … cats." May I make a suggestion? "Two mums." Mahesh is shocked. Gary told me that Mahesh knew, although he didn't want me to know because he'd 'lose my respect forever'. At the time I said, "That's okay. Just don't tell anyone else." Now I'm not so sure. Gary's not my friend any more. Bastard.

Finally I got sick of hiding. That's like admitting there's something wrong with my parents, and there's nothing wrong with my parents. They're nicer than most of my friends' parents. Billy's dad chugalugs beer and sits in front of the footy while his mum does the housework. Todd's parents are divorced and he hates his dad with a vengeance.

There's another absentee note in the roll. Of course I get the same again. Not a spark of originality in their insults.

"Who's Ms Maaaaarsfield?"

"She's my mum."

"Then who's Ms Wilde?"

"She's my mum too. God you people are stupid." He sits in silence. Fuck this. I stand, yelling, "Does everybody want to see? Look! Gay! Queer! Dykes! Homosexuals!" Want to walk out of class. Go home. But I don't have the guts. I sit, my face reddening. But I feel good, deep in my gut.

A few weeks later. Lesbian-insult free weeks. Freeman tries again. "Two muuuuuums." I sit without speaking. "It's not as much fun teasing you now you've admitted it. I thought it would be more fun, but it's not." Next late note, I'm cool.

MAEVE MARSDEN

Have you got two mums?

Maeve Marsden is 11 years old

I was at school, playing tips with my friends and my little sister was there too. I saw a boy who was in year six coming towards me.

"Hey," he said, "you got two mums, don't ya?"

"No," I said.

"Yes you do," my sister said, who at the time didn't realise that this kid could give me a really hard time if he found out about my parents. I kept insisting that I did not have two mothers and my little sister kept saying that I did. After a while he went away, probably planning to spread the news. I was really angry with my sister, but afterwards I decided that it wasn't her fault.

I was still really angry with Tim Smith (the boy who was teasing me) so as soon as I went back to class I went and had a talk with my teacher. She went and had a talk with Mrs Johnson, Tim's teacher.

The next day one of Tim's friends came over and gave me an apology letter. Although he had gotten one of his friends to give it to me and the letter did sound like a copy of what the teacher had told him he should include, oh well, what else could I do?

That afternoon I was on a message. One of the male teachers in my school is gay and when I got to his classroom he asked about the incident with Tim the day before. I told him that everything had been sorted out and that I had an apology letter, but it felt good that he had made it his business to find out and ask about it because he knew that I had two mums.

I am not ashamed about my family. In fact I would not want things any differently. I hope nothing like that ever happens again.

JAY WALKER

Elton John's Cousin
(or Come out, come out, wherever you are)

Jay Walker is 10 years old

"Yes, I know I'm a wooss, a girl, a freak, a guinea pig, call me what ever you want!" That's what I'll tell everyone at school today. My name is Jay Walker and I'm almost ten. My *mums* are lesbians and my *dad* is gay. I was born by artificial insemination. I'm not a test-tube baby, or a tar-baby, I'm a jar-baby.

I'm afraid. Afraid of what? I hear you say. I'm afraid of coming out, I'm afraid of what the kids at school will do to me. And I *know* what they'll do to me as well. First, they'll bash me, then they'll dunny dunk me, then who knows what they'll do to me! For all I know my friends could all turn against me, or maybe the big bully of the school, who is tough and fat, would start calling me Elton John's cousin. That's his favourite phrase for poofs. At least I'd be able to call him 'Sumo wrestler's son'.

Some boys think that I'm a poof because I play with girls. But I just say, "I play with girls, you play with boys. Who's the real poof?" Chris is a good friend of mine, but he likes to be with the crowd. One day I saw him talking to Richard, who said, "Hey Chris, yesterday I saw these totally real lesos, and they had their arms around each other!" and Chris said, "Yeah, and I saw this total poof on Monday!" Once, in the playground, when Lila and Jenny hugged each other after a fight, I heard a boy in year six sing to the Praise Mayonnaise tune "L.E.S.B.I.A.N. spells lesbian."

That's why today, like every other day, I'm going to try to get it all over with. I walk into school and see someone. It's Danny.

"Hey Danny!" I say.

"Yeah?" he answers.

61

But then something in my brain goes tick and I end up saying, "Got any new basketball cards?" Somehow he isn't the best person to tell first.

Then I see Jenny playing handball. She's the leader of the gang I hang around with at lunchtime and little lunch, and she's in my Scripture.

I start to walk towards her, but then I remember what her father looks like, big, mean and tattooed! And a Christian. Jenny always used to be a real Christian too, and when people hurt themselves or it was a rainy day, she'd say things like, "God'll make it better," or "Don't worry, God's looking upon you right now." But Jenny likes to be with the crowd, too, and if someone said to her, "Lesbian mums, ugh, that's gross," she'd say that too. It's harder than I thought! By the end of the day I haven't told anyone!

As my mum Cathy drives me home, she asks me if I was any more successful today at trying to tell people about my lesbian mums. I say, "Mission bloody unsuccessful once again."

Then Cathy says, "Jay, why are you trying to tell every one about us when you know you'll get hurt?" But I don't answer.

That night I have the worst dream I've ever had in my entire life, I swear it was the worst nightmare ever anybody could have. I dreamt that I was in assembly and Mr Bean was the headmaster. All of a sudden the assembly presenters announced that it was time for anyone to make an announcement, about anything they have to tell you. For some reason my legs seemed to stand up without me making them do it. And then, when I got out the front, my mouth magically moved and said, "Hi, my name is Jay, and my mums are lesbians."

Everybody's face looked weird, especially the principal's. He was making the stupidest noises and expressions you ever saw. And then Stevie in Year 5 croaked, "Let's get the poof!"

If Stevie wants to put someone down, he always says things like, "Ugh, that kid's got a gay germ!" (The dickhead thinks all the girls love him, and that he's some perfect super-guy because he's good at softball, and I only play korf-ball, which is actually more recreational.) They all ran at me with chairs and pocket-knives. Stevie's mum was in the back row, and she was wiping her clothes as if something horrible was crawling all over her, and I knew what she was doing. She was trying to sweep off the so-called 'gay germ'. I heard her saying, "Imagine, I let them come to our house yesterday — I should have known better!"

Stevie comes up to the front of the crowd, and holds up this medicine bottle in my face, and says, "It's a gay germ cure — it immunises you against the gay disease!" Everyone drops their chairs and pocket-knives and starts to queue up behind him to have a sip of the potion. Then he says to me, "Just imagine, one little sip and you'd be free ... free ... freeeeeeeeeeeeeee ..."

I wake up screaming, and go to the bathroom to have a drink of water, and Alana (my other mother) says, "It's about time you woke up! I've tried to wake you, but you just lie there snoring your head off. The bell will go in five minutes, so you better get your arse outa here!" I decide to keep quiet about my dream, in case my mums think I need to see a child psychologist.

I pack my homework, get dressed in my sports outfit, throw my lunch into my bag and make sure I've got my hat. Then it's off for another day of school. At little lunch Lila suddenly jumps out and says, "Hey, Jay, my mum says your mums are lesbians, is it true?"

That's when I get mad, and I mean mad.

"Shut up you bitch of a shitburger with maggots on the side! Tell your mom who has five children and no husband because he ran away when you were five that she shouldn't go making accusations like that because we could take her to court, OKAY?"

(God, my mums are going to say I'm denying them thrice, like Peter in the Bible. Thank Christ they're not *really* religious — except that they almost know the Bible off by heart. Gee, parents can be a pain in the arse, sometimes.)

But after that I feel happy because Jenny kicks Lila out of our gang. Maybe Jenny wouldn't be such a bad person to tell after all ... ???????

JULIE BEAUCHAMP

Relationship Counselling and the Lesbian Family

In an organisation like ours (Relationships Australia, formerly Marriage Guidance New South Wales), it initially took me by surprise when I had my first session as counsellor to lesbian partners. Even more surprising at the time was that the presenting problem was domestic violence. I have since seen several lesbian couples, and come to realise that violence *does* occur in some lesbian relationships. Furthermore, some lesbian couples have consciously chosen to avoid lesbian counselling services because of possible confidentiality limitations within a close-knit community.

Whether a predominantly heterosexually-focussed organisation and straight couple/family therapists can be effective with lesbian clients needs to be seriously considered. Generally speaking, if therapists see being lesbian as the problem, or if they naively believe that being a lesbian makes no difference, then they will be ineffectual (if not damaging!) in working with this client group. Whilst the literature dealing with couple and family issues for lesbian couples is not extensive, there is sufficient for therapists to be adequately informed about their suitability to work with lesbian couples, eg adequate training in relationship focussed therapies, awareness of homophobia and its many forms, understanding issues of social context and feminist theory in family therapy. Potential clients also need to do their homework, approaching the first few sessions as a trial period to see whether the therapist has an understanding of issues faced by lesbian couples and parents.

In writing about lesbian relationships as I've experienced them as a counsellor, I have had some reservations about publication. My reservations are similar to those cited in the literature as reasons why the lesbian community overlooks or denies the reality of domestic violence among some of its members. That is, would publication of such information give ammunition to those who are anti-gay and anti-feminist? Would I be challenged on issues of gender politics, and for exposing that lesbians, too, experience difficulties with negotiation, co-operation, power, equality and even violence in intimate relationships?

Recently, I have been somewhat encouraged by the appearance of a number of newspaper articles highlighting difficulties in practice and policy, mainly in government spheres which affect gay couples. The latest described the discrimination homosexual families experience because they are not recognised as 'family' under the law:

> For example, a same sex couple with kids can be denied the family rate of medical insurance ... They are not regarded as next of kin when it comes to granting permission of emergency medical treatment, being able to see a dying loved one in hospital, authorising a coroner's inquest or inheriting the estate of a partner who has died. Nor are they entitled to worker's compensation if a partner has died, or the superannuation payout.
> (The Sydney Morning Herald: 27/8/94)

These issues need to be addressed by governments and legal bodies. Clearly, non-traditional families are entitled to resources commonly available to 'traditional families'.

Marriage Guidance New South Wales recently changed its name to Relationships Australia to reflect more realistically the breadth of counselling and educational services provided, as well as to acknowledge the diversity of our client base. However, 'gay and lesbian-headed families are still something of an anomaly in our society — there's never been a sitcom about one — and there are few role models for them to follow' (*Networker*, p.46). The number of lesbian couples and lesbian-headed families we see is still quite small; they do exist, however, and the personal and emotional costs of remaining hidden and not having access to legal rights, social and health/welfare services, must be taken seriously.

The following story about Karen and Donna (not their real names) will highlight some of the significant issues for lesbian parents, and lesbian-headed step-families with adolescents. Donna is 34 and Karen 46. They have been in a relationship for two and a half years, having known each other as friends for two years prior to that. Karen has two teenage children — Cathy, aged 16 and beginning year 11, and Stephen, aged 14, in year 9 at the same local high school.

Karen separated from her husband four years ago after a long history of being the victim of physical violence. The children witnessed these episodes of violence but were not physically assaulted themselves. Karen had attempted to separate from her husband on several occasions during their 23 years of marriage but she had gone back to him for a variety of reasons, including financial hardship and his continued threats.

After the last episode of violence Karen and the children had hurriedly moved out of their large family home, taking only their clothes and a few household items. Because of her husband's financial control, which prevented her having access to bank accounts, Karen had to borrow money from friends and family for bond, rent, food and beds. A friend lent her a car for two months and she was able to secure a full-time job, despite the fact that she had only worked occasionally part-time since Cathy was born.

Donna had left home at the age of 16 owing to her own father's physical violence. She had a chequered employment career, and her longest intimate relationship had been with a woman for seven years — this relationship had ended 12 months prior to meeting Karen. Donna had lesbian relationships exclusively, and had been open about her sexual orientation since meeting Karen and her children.

When they met, it seemed that Donna's understanding of Karen's experience of violence and her willingness to help out practically came at just the right time. Karen appreciated this support, particularly as her family lived some distance from her, and many of Karen's friends had drifted away, either because they found out about her husband's abuse or because they were frustrated by her returning to him on previous occasions. Cathy and Stephen also enjoyed Donna's friendship and her support of their mother, and began feeling that they could get on with their lives without constant tension in the house and the fear of their father's frequent outbursts. They even heard their mother laugh for the first time in years.

Even though leaving had provided some respite from the fear and violence, there were several episodes when Donna was visiting, where Karen's husband would make threatening phone calls. Also, Donna had been followed one evening after leaving Karen's house and her car tyres had been slashed. After one such incident, Karen took out an apprehended violence order against her husband. Subsequently, the harassment lessened, but Karen, Donna and the children became vigilant and constantly feared further abuse.

Karen filed for divorce and instructed her legal representative to file for property settlement. Some weeks after instituting this action, the harassment began again with Karen again receiving threatening phone calls. The police were called a number of times.

During this period Donna seemed to be the one who was more 'cool-headed' and kept the family hopeful that, once the divorce was finalised, the harassment would subside. As a measure of seeking more support during this crisis, and because their relationship was developing, Karen asked Donna if she would come and live with them. Donna agreed, particularly as she was spending most of her free time with Karen and the children, and had come to feel like part of the family.

Cathy and Stephen had thought for some time that their mother's relationship with Donna was more than a passing friendship. Before Karen asked her to move in, she sat down with the children and told them that she and Donna had decided to live as partners. Initially, both children expressed surprise and concern about their mother's choice to enter into a lesbian relationship. Cathy openly expressed her reservations and Stephen seemed more thoughtful, but they both agreed that Donna had become important to them, and they supported Karen in asking Donna to move in. Cathy had come to rely on Donna to help with her maths homework, and Stephen shared Donna's favourite past-time — fishing.

When Donna and Karen came for couple therapy, they had been living together for two years and were experiencing a number of stressful changes. Donna had been unemployed for six weeks, having been retrenched, and Karen had started attending tech at night three months prior to Donna's retrenchment. Karen went to tech straight from work on two evenings per week. Cathy was about to do her trial HSC exams, and Stephen had been suspended from school after being caught smoking while truanting.

On the recommendation of a friend, Karen suggested they come to counselling as a couple because they were arguing more seriously about managing the children. There had been one incident where Donna had slapped Karen and pushed her against a wall. This had scared them both. However, Karen minimised this violence and felt the more important issue was Donna being unreasonable about restrictions and punishments. Donna said she felt undermined in dealing with Cathy and Stephen, particularly when Karen stepped in and tried to mediate between her and the children over acceptable standards of domestic chores and homework completion.

Several issues were raised in therapy. These included very common step-parenting matters, the effects of violence and abuse on each member of the family, parenting adolescents, and the establishment of a new relationship. The following were identified, over the course of several counselling sessions, as the 'hot' issues Karen and Donna struggled with the most:

• When there was a crisis, eg an episode of harassment from Karen's ex-husband, the family (including Donna) would become closer. Once the crisis passed, arguments between Donna and the children seemed to increase.

• Donna felt resentful that Karen spent time away from home, leaving her to supervise the children. Like any step-parent dealing with adolescents for the first time, Donna struggled with differentiating between her roles of friend and confidante on the one hand, and responsible adult/authority figure on the other.

• Donna felt excluded from the relationship between Karen and the children and particularly from Karen's relationship with Cathy, which seemed to strengthen when Cathy was making career decisions or seeing a new boyfriend.

• Karen felt she needed to be more lenient towards the children because of the trauma they had expressed in witnessing domestic violence, and because of her feelings of guilt in breaking up the family and expecting the children to accept her new relationship. Karen felt Donna's demands for attention and private couple time were unreasonable if it meant being unavailable to the children.

• Donna's retrenchment and Karen's absences owing to study exacerbated Donna's feelings of resentment. She felt Karen 'had it easy' by having been married and receiving her share of the property settlement, and in many respects Donna saw Karen advance (financially, emotionally, academically, socially) while she felt increasingly burdened and disempowered. Donna was also fearful of losing the relationship with Karen and her position in the family.

• Donna was increasingly frustrated that Karen had still not told her parents and siblings about their relationship after living together for two years. She felt Karen was somehow ashamed of her, and even began to doubt Karen's ongoing commitment to the relationship and lesbianism.

• Karen had begun to feel Donna was making more emotional and sexual demands, rather than providing support and practical help in the way she had done during their friendship.

As the therapist, it was important for me to identify practical issues and assist Karen and Donna to deal with current stresses. In addition, for any lasting changes to occur within the relationship, some of the historical and emotional issues needed to be understood and resolved. My first priority was to help Karen and Donna establish some safety procedures for themselves so that, whatever they argued about, they were confident that violence would not recur. This included helping them identify the emotional triggers to avoid, and employing strategies like agreeing to take time out when arguments escalated. These were short-term solutions which would be needed less as the underlying issues which led to conflict were gradually resolved.

The next step was to identify concerns which could be addressed by practical solutions and compromise. The first task was for Karen and

Donna to negotiate their own 'bottom lines' in terms of acceptable and non-acceptable behaviour of the children. As a way of developing agreement and compromise, they set up a daily parenting 'meeting' where they as a couple discussed managing various issues concerning the children. They also agreed to read some self-help material about parents surviving adolescence!

Karen agreed to set time aside on a daily and weekly basis as 'couple only time'. Donna also decided to meet some of her own needs by re-establishing contact with friends and starting a daily walking/exercise program. She felt more motivated to look for work once Karen agreed to go through the employment advertisements with her at the weekend.

Even though Donna still felt she often came second to the children with Karen, she was able to accept Cathy's need for more of Karen's attention at this time. Donna decided to focus her parenting energies more on Stephen, and Karen informed Stephen's year co-ordinator that Donna (as family friend) would be monitoring his attendance. Whilst Stephen initially protested at this 'surveillance' and demonstrated some resistance to reconnecting with Donna (after feeling she had become 'stressed out and heavy' with him), he seemed to respond to her increased involvement with him. Donna was particularly sensitive to Stephen's concerns that her increased contact with the school would lead to teachers and friends finding out about the relationship. In a session with the four family members present, these fears were discussed, as was the issue of secrets — what was important to be kept just between Karen and Donna? what could be shared between family? and what information would be kept within the family vs shared outside the family?

Once some of these tangible matters had been addressed, the more difficult and frightening issues between Donna and Karen needed to be tackled. Much of Donna's frustration with Karen's 'soft' parenting style was alleviated following several sessions where the effects of violence were discussed. Each woman's experience of violence was understood in detail, and how this then affected the way they saw Stephen and Cathy's response to their father's violence.

It was during one of these sessions that Donna blurted out that she thought Karen had only entered the relationship with her because she was a 'vehicle of escape' from the violence, rather than out of genuine physical attraction. What followed was a number of sessions exploring how each of them remembered the circumstances around their getting together and how these circumstances, whilst helpful in establishing the relationship, also planted the seeds of doubt.

Karen acknowledged that she thought Donna valued being in a family and being 'useful' much more than she valued being in a relationship with 'a middle-aged, overweight housewife'. She also realised that distancing from Donna and supporting Cathy helped her avoid her fear that lesbian relationships were unreliable, and that Donna would look for someone younger, sooner or later.

Donna found it extremely difficult to understand Karen's ongoing reluctance to 'come out' to her family; however, she was gradually able to accept Karen's position (without condoning it). She continued to question Karen's commitment to lesbianism, usually at times when she was needing Karen's attention. Being aware of this enabled Donna to use her 'doubts' as a signal, and it led the way to a difficult but useful broader discussion about the enormous pressures on lesbian couples and lesbian-headed families. As Markowitz has established:

> The fact that same-sex couples have to balance stress in so many systems at once — their own families of origin, their relationship, the gay/lesbian community, their ethnic or religious communities, and mainstream society — makes their efforts at forming a family an impressive juggling act. And the complexity of a relationship between people with the same gender socialisation can create further confusion and conflict, yet the problem may not be evident to the straight therapist. (Networker, p.33)

Owing to the complexity of this relationship and family circumstances, the therapy continued on a fortnightly basis for several months. A number of external and emotional changes took place. Donna started part-time work and training with the public service. Karen completed her studies and began working as a welfare officer. Cathy passed her HSC and took a year off to travel interstate with friends. Stephen continued to truant and, as a result of his schoolwork deteriorating, Karen arranged for him to re-establish contact with his father via a restricted access agreement.

For Donna and Karen, balancing the need for closeness and reassurance with the maintenance of a 'separate self' was a constant struggle. Closeness to the point of fusion is often what makes lesbian relationships so committed and long lasting, but isolation, lack of individual space and separate identity can create a volatile situation. Whilst Karen and Donna were still together at the termination of therapy, their relationship had become more an intimate friendship with fewer crises and a greater balance between meeting each others' needs, and their own individual growth. They were supporting each other in the face of an 'empty nest' — with Cathy living away and Stephen spending more time with his friends, and every second weekend with his father.

Despite the initial fears about seeking relationship counselling, Karen and Donna made good use of their sessions to deal with the difficult crisis issues and then later as a resource or 'safety zone' where they could tackle issues that felt insoluble on their own. Over time they developed a greater understanding and practical skills, both of which enabled them to deal with issues as they arose, in an increasingly effective manner.

Bibliography

Crawford, S. (1988) 'Cultural Context as a Factor in the Expansion of Therapeutic Conversation with Lesbian Families', *Journal of Strategic and Systemic Therapies,* vol.7#3, p.2.

Dahlheimer, D. and Feigal, J. (Jan/Feb. 1991) 'Bridging the Gap', *Networker,* pp.44-53.

Eldridge, N.S. (1987) 'Gender Issues in Counselling Same-Sex Couples', *Professional Psychology - Research and Practice,* vol.18 no.6, pp.567-572.

Hersch, P. (Jan/Feb. 1991) 'Secret Lives', *Networker,* pp.37-43.

Josefowitz Siegel, R. (1987) 'Beyond Homophobia: Learning to Work with Lesbian Clients', *Women and Therapy,* vol.6 (1-2), pp.125-133.

Krestan, J. and Bepko, C. (1980) 'The Problem of Fusion in the Lesbian Relationship', *Family Process,* p.277.

Markowitz, L.M. (Jan/Feb. 1991) 'Homosexuality: Are We Still in the Dark?', *Networker,* pp.27 ff.

Pies, C. (1987) *Lesbians Choosing Children: The Use of Social Group Work in Maintaining and Strengthening the Primary Relationship.* The Haworth Press.

Rich, A. (1982) *Compulsory Heterosexuality and Lesbian Existence.* Antelope Publications.

Roth, S. (July 1985) 'Psychotherapy with Lesbian Couples: Individual Issues, Female Socialization and the Social Context', *Journal of Marital and Family Therapy,* vol.11, no.3, pp.273-86.

KERRY SAWTELL

No Absolute Rights

I was in the Family Court the other day. I was acting for the mother in an application for custody of her five year old daughter. The father was there and he was also applying for custody of his daughter. The father's allegation was that the mother is a drug addict and the child would be better off with him. The mother's allegation was that the father is dysfunctional and holds unorthodox religious views and that the child was better off with her. I wonder what the child thinks?

I am 37 years old and a lawyer practising primarily in family law. I was married for 13 years and came out as a lesbian three years ago. I have two children, a boy aged seven and a girl aged six. My partner is 36 years old and we've been living together for about nine months. The children live with us for one week, then with their father for a week, and so the arrangement goes on. This basically works because we all live about five minutes apart; all parents do their best to reinforce the love and security of the children and hold the view that the children are not a single individual's property to be used as a bargaining chip in their parents' lives.

Basically the children's lives have been affected, but we have tried to minimise that effect. For instance, they have had to adjust to their mother and father having new partners; and to the fact that there are now two other adults in their lives who play a role in parenting, including supervision. I believe it is important to emphasise my love for each child so that they don't feel threatened by my love for my partner. This has been made easy because my partner has shown a real love and interest in the children, and so they feel secure. I have also found it necessary to explain to my children that even though I may have moved away from their father, I was not about to leave them; that, because their father loves them and they love their father, we all needed to work out a situation where they could spend time with each parent. The children have slipped into this arrangement with ease and know that it is flexible yet stable.

Because of the shared situation we have in our family, I believe they see their parents' partners as close adult friends that they can rely on. The children have a broader exposure to life and will learn to deal with situations that exposure will bring. The support of those around them will help them.

Sounds idyllic, doesn't it? It wasn't always that way. Their father battled with his own homophobia. He was concerned that 'his' children would be exposed to weird, unnatural behaviour and that I didn't have their best interests at heart. He argued that I chose to be a lesbian. My reply to that was: "Yes, I did choose to follow a path that was natural for me, and thereby chose not to deny my true sexuality." This no longer seems to be a major issue, but has been replaced by his concern that the children come from a 'broken home'. I actually have difficulty with that one, but pacify myself with the thought that we do not live in a perfect world.

To get through these stages requires commitment, sensitivity, acceptance of others and communication. These are not always possible, and during the emotional upheaval never easy.

What does the law say on homosexuality and children?

In 1977 the Family Court of Western Australia awarded the mother, who was living in a lesbian relationship, custody of her two girls aged seven and three, and her son aged five, in circumstances where their father drank heavily. The mother was involved in the children's school work and activities and was able to care for them, day to day, more competently than the father. The mother was living with a woman, openly sharing a bedroom with her and intended to continue doing so if awarded custody. In granting custody to the mother the Court said, "… Nor do I consider that the behaviour of the mother with her partner would affect the children's normal development towards adulthood, in terms of being influenced towards that course of behaviour."

The 'apparent' homosexuality of the father was considered in a 1978 decision where the Court ordered that the mother have custody of her four year old son, and that the father have access which did not include overnight access.

In 1979 a case considered the lesbianism of the mother. The day to day care and control of a 14 year old daughter was given to the mother, who was living in a lesbian relationship; the child wished to live with the mother and was unhappy living with the father and his new wife. The Court held that it was entitled to consider the reality of the distress of the child and to see this against the unsubstantiated risks which she might be subjected to should she reside with her mother. The evidence of the mother and her partner showed that they had a balanced outlook and an awareness of the problems that their relationship might cause.

Again in 1979 the Family Court in Western Australia gave custody of a three year old daughter to the father and not to the mother, who was living in a lesbian relationship, and where 'expert' witnesses gave opinions as to the effects of homosexuality. In respect of 'expert' evidence introduced during the trial, the Court said that at the present time there had not been sufficient or adequate research yet done into the question of the effect on a child being brought up in a homosexual household. However, the Court was of the opinion that at that time in Australia there was an actual risk of stigmatisation, with possible consequences of faulty personality development, if a child were to be brought up in a lesbian household.

In 1983 the Family Court said: 'Where a homosexual parent is seeking an order for the custody of children, or indeed, if a homosexual parent seeks an order for access to children, the following are matters which a Court must take into account in arriving at its decision:

- *Whether children raised by their homosexual parent may themselves become homosexual or whether such an event is likely.*
- *Whether the child of a homosexual parent could be stigmatised by peer groups, particularly if the parent is known in the community as a homosexual.*
- *Whether a homosexual parent would show the same love and responsibility as a heterosexual parent.*
- *Whether homosexual parents will give a balanced sex education to their children and take a balanced approach to sexual matters.*
- *Whether or not children should be made aware of their parents' sexual preferences.*
- *Whether children need a parent of the same sex to model upon.*
- *Whether children need both a male and a female parent figure.*
- *The attitude of the homosexual parent to religion, particularly if the doctrines, tenets and beliefs of the parties' church are opposed to homosexuality.*

In that case the Court, considering those factors, awarded custody of four children aged two to eight years to the mother, who was living in a lesbian relationship. It appeared to the Court that the mother was able to provide better care and arrangements and was the custodian to be preferred, notwithstanding the fact that she was living, with the children, in an openly lesbian relationship.

And finally, in 1992, the Court granted custody of a nine year old boy to his father who was living in a permanent homosexual relationship. In doing so, the Court found that the morality and the sexual orientation of the parents are only two of the important factors to be considered, but they are limited in their effect as to what relevance they have, directly or indirectly, to the welfare of the child. The parent's lifestyle is of no relevance without consideration of its consequences on the child's well-being. Homosexuality is only relevant if it affects parenting ability, or the welfare of the child.

So, it is the welfare of the child that is the primary consideration in all matters relating to children. The child might have a particular view but, depending upon her age, this is only one of the many factors a Court will consider. The older the child, the greater the weight the Court will place on the child's wishes.

Artificial insemination presents new circumstances.

Chris was 33 years old when she and her partner, Kate, had their child. Chris conceived by means of impregnating herself with sperm from a donor whom they knew but, once he provided the sperm, had nothing further to do with in terms of the child.

Kate participated in Chris' pregnancy and assisted in the home birth. For six years they raised James together, sharing all the tasks associated with a mother and her child. Although Chris was the biological parent, Kate was, and still is, a major influence in James' life.

For reasons of their own, when James was six, Kate and Chris separated and James became a pawn in their separation. Chris argued that Kate 'had no right to James' and refused Kate the joy of seeing him. You will see that this one-sided view doesn't even consider what James' needs might be. The law would say that it is James' right to have 'at least access' to Kate, even to the point of ordering Chris to suppress her hostile feelings for Kate, as far as James is concerned, and support and co-operate in his emotional adjustment to the new situation.

After many hours of mediation, Chris consented to Kate's having access to James. Apart from appealing to the better judgment of Chris, the legalities were put to her. That is, the child has a right of access to continue, and to develop, a relationship with Kate.

You can almost hear the argument which might develop here. 'But she isn't a parent; she is not a biological parent.' The obvious reply is: 'Biology has nothing to do with it. Don't interpret the word "parent" so narrowly.'

Section 63C(1) of the Family Law Act, 1975 provides that any person *who has an interest in the welfare of the child* may commence an application in the Court for custody, guardianship or access to the child.

Section 64(2) of that Act provides that, in relation to custody, guardianship or access to a child the Court may make one or more of the following orders:

- *an order placing the child in the custody of any person ... (whether or not that person is a parent);*
- *an order placing the child in the guardianship of any person ... (whether or*

not that person is a parent);

• *an order granting to any person ... (whether or not that person is a parent) rights of access to the child.*

You can see that the Act allows Kate to apply for custody, guardianship or access to James, notwithstanding that she is not one of James' biological parents. The qualification is that Kate must have a real interest in the child. This can be supported by evidence of a long-term relationship and care of the child. If Kate had been the primary care-giver of James, she might have been successful in obtaining an order for custody of James. In short, there is no absolute parental right to a child.

This concept of 'no absolute parental right to a child' extends to the 'wish' a parent might make in their Will. They might nominate whom they wish to be guardian of their child. Legally, this 'wish' is only an indication of the parent's desire and is not enforceable. It is only either the Family Court of Australia or the Supreme Court, by way of adoption proceedings, which can make orders (which are enforceable) of guardianship and custody.

If Chris had died, Kate could make an application to the Family Court for custody of James as an 'interested person'.

Even though legislation provides certain rights, don't naively assume you are home and hosed. There are many competing interests and factors a Court will consider in relation to children. Needless to say, there is not room in this article to present a comprehensive review of the law as it relates to children. In fact, the law may change with the passing of a Bill currently before Federal Parliament. The Family Law Reform Bill, 1994 has been introduced, and its aim is to establish a new approach dealing with children. It focuses on 'parental responsibility for the care, welfare and development of children', rather than giving parents any rights to custody and access.

The Bill makes clear that children have the right to know and be cared for by both their parents; that children have the right to regular contact with both their parents *and any other person who is significant to their care, welfare and development.*

If you find yourself in the position of Kate or myself, don't despair entirely. Seek assistance, be assured of your own position and, if you have the courage and (unfortunately necessary, sometimes) the financial backing, don't give up.

MARILYN MITCHELL

Broadening the Options:
The Family and the Bisexual Lesbian

When I was a child, I always fantasised about being a (valiant) wounded soldier or cowboy (not cowgirl). I never played with stiff (stupid, ugly) dolls, only my floppy old teddy, who was not pretty but who had character.

My mother arranged for me to go to an all-girls' school, as she did not want me to become pregnant to a boy upon entering high school. So I went to the girls' school — and soon met and fell in love with another girl, with whom I had an affair which lasted four years, until we both completed the HSC, in 1969. At that time, we were heart-breakingly torn apart, for she was sent to a country teachers' college, whilst I was posted to the one in Sydney.

In my teenaged ignorance, I had feared that I could become pregnant to Jay through genital contact — later on I had even relished the thought of bearing her children.

However, timid, naive, aware of societal norms, ignorant of the homosexual community's whereabouts, on the rebound from this relationship and with the match-making assistance of my mother, I soon married, as a 'child-bride' aged nineteen. This was in 1971. I did very much want (unlimited) children, and so did my husband-to-be, who was Chinese.

By the age of twenty-seven I was a teacher, had three young children under the age of five — and suffered my first admission to a psychiatric hospital. Over the years, Jay and I saw each other from time to time. For a long while she was earnestly pursuing parenthood — hoping to conceive via a monthly meeting with a male friend in Sydney. He was the brother of a lesbian friend, and was agreeable to donating his sperm to a worthy cause. Unfortunately for Jay, the endeavour had to be abandoned. She always told me that she hankered after a child after having a long-time relationship with a woman with a handicapped child, for whom she helped to care when the child was an infant. Jay took to my children, too, when they were wee infants, and vice versa. She had moved on into a fully lesbian existence, and in addition had an aggressively jealous girlfriend (who toted a shotgun). At one stage, prior to this, we had toyed with the idea of her moving into our home; however, my husband thought that we would be sharing her.

Anyhow, with my diagnosis of manic-depressive illness and following a number of breakdowns and hospitalisations, my husband soon left. The psychiatrist's orders had been "No more children — it's genetic." And so began many years of attempted and failed relationships, firstly with men, and only much later, with women.

I realised that I was a 'bisexual lesbian' when I first heard that term used by the poet Dorothy Porter about herself in the late 1980s. I regard myself as a bisexual lesbian because I think, feel and act like one — I swear, I like driving a car hard and fast, I wear boots and bush shirts and men's ties, have never liked frills or bright colours, cooking or sewing, fussing over nails or my hair. I do wear a little makeup and lipstick and dress well — but then lipstick dykes are in! I love poetry and art above all else (and walking, reading, copperwork and leatherwork), and sex is a driving force.

During my marriage and throughout the years of having relationships with several guys, I always sought (in an underground kind of way) union with another woman. However, these friends and other teachers to whom I was attracted were invariably 'straight' and turned me down. Thus, lack of opportunity prevented my coupling with another woman for over a decade.

And there was always the fear of being declared an unfit mother and having my children taken away. I had to be very careful lest my ex-husband turn vindictive and have them removed, such were the laws of the time.

Thus, when I was in my late thirties, I began to no longer feel able to suffer this great absence and urge in my life. I became aware of the gay and lesbian scene through a number in the telephone book. Surreptitiously, I made enquiries. There was a breakthrough case in Western Australia which I heard about on the radio where a homosexual guy won custody of his children. My son, in whom I had confided, maturely applauded this victory with me. He was about fourteen at the time.

Interestingly, my son has always been the child who has unequivocally supported me throughout this changeover. It is my two younger daughters who have at times been ambivalent about my bisexuality/lesbianism.

Earlier, I had remarried briefly but for the wrong reasons — the sex, the money, but mainly believing that my children needed a father! The domestic violence that ensued soon convinced me otherwise. I found that men did not want to father another man's children — this conflict of filling a parental role has not arisen with my female lovers, however. Rather, there have been some personality clashes or ideological differences. In addition, in attempting a bisexual existence, my second husband also thought he would 'crack onto' Jay, when she stayed over with us, making it a threesome. Neither Jay nor I had inclinations in that regard — not with my first husband and not with the second one either.

Never being one to rush into relationships, being selective and cautious by nature, it was to be a year or so before more than basic amorous contact took place. At this time, too, I was starting to learn more about lesbians, lesbianism and the scene, and to break the news gently (but firmly) to my children — aware of their delicate but still receptive early adolescent stage of development. I explained that 'all love is good', whether it is between male and male, male and female or female and female. They began to get used to the idea of my bisexual lesbianism. I think they were a little bit frightened — they asked, "Why don't you keep going out with — ?" (a male). Later on, they'd be nominating preferences with regard to my girlfriends.

Later, I brought home a lesbian friend or two, to let them meet lesbians and to see that they were also decent 'normal' human beings — not alien, perverted freaks. The children, aged nine, eleven and fourteen at that time, were themselves on the threshold of their sexual existence, so it was a critical period for all of us. Things might have been more difficult at a later date.

I had always preferred older women. Perhaps I wanted a wise and cuddly mother. I had never been into young girls — there was a kind of intellectual sterility there. I met an older woman who was into 'young virgins' like me, and who soon had me into bed. I had not at first been attracted to her, but did later fall in love. She had quite a forceful, dominating approach. However, I think Ellen, a teacher, was somewhat disappointed with my body, suffering as it had three births and two miscarriages in my twelve years of marriage. She told me that she liked 'young women's bodies', although she was sixty (with a fast, silver sports car). Her keen interest in my children later became a worry — her comments on their developing bodies and legs, on my young daughter's nipples showing through her night-dress, etc. only later took on a more worrying meaning. Once, she told me that she had fantasized about having sex with my children, even my son. I became confused. But she solved the problem by quickly tiring of me, and moving on to another much younger woman.

After this experience, I decided that I wanted a relationship with a woman who also had children. Kris' three children and mine related well to each other and to both of us. We shared common interests. However, I soon felt overwhelmed and drained by her demands, and by the excesses of our involvement. I needed more space and solitude, especially in view of my mental illness, now re-diagnosed as schizo-affective disorder. After less than a year the relationship ended. The saddest thing for me was no longer being allowed to continue seeing *her* children. And I suspect that this was the case for them, too, as I heard that they asked after me. I felt that it had been a positive and significant situation for all of our children with regard to their understanding and acceptance of lesbians, especially since her children had been copping some flak at school.

Then came Jan, a younger woman with whom I had an affair. She had always been a lesbian, for twenty plus years, and liked my boyish figure and appearance. Unlike Kris, she was obsessive about concealing any evidence of our lesbianism, to the extent of wearing skirts and high heels.

This relationship, too, failed because I became progressively more damaged by it. *My* inclination was to be gentle but open (at last) with regard to my (bi)sexuality. I regarded touching, kissing, cuddling and holding hands as affection that was natural and 'good', especially as far as being observed by my children was concerned. I did not believe that lesbianism ought to be understood by them to be something perverted or mysterious that two women did in the bedroom with the door closed. I also wanted them to see the caring, loving companionship side of it too. This seemed a more balanced and accurate depiction of being gay. No matter how much we discussed it, Jan would never accept my feelings and totally rejected any attempts at affection outside the bedroom. As well, there was some mutual jealousy — Jan was not really into children, and practically came to fisticuffs with my eldest daughter on several occasions. She simply did not tolerate children well.

I, in turn, could not just suddenly switch on without these prelim- inaries, into a raging sex kitten when the door was shut. So as a result I gradually became sexually and psychologically shattered. This was clearly not healthy, so I eventually broke off this relationship (to the disappointment of my younger daughter!)

Periodically, homophobic ideas have been expressed by the children — something they may have heard at school or seen on television. For my part, I have tried to balance the argument by drawing attention to positive aspects of homosexuality/bisexuality and by correcting misin- formation. They had never liked their step-father or — ("She was a bitch!") but had liked most of their 'uncles' and my female lovers/ friends. It was usually a matter of personal compatibility that mattered, not the sex of the friend/lover.

For some time now I have been involved in a steady relationship with a woman, Julie. This contains all the gentleness, emotional closeness and natural empathy that I had so long desired. My present girlfriend is both very sexy and very sensitive. We share this, and also a psychiatric disability — a very cohesive factor in our case, as we have both suffered greatly from rejection by past lovers who were mentally and physically well.

One of the confusing (and surprising) issues that has arisen with the children has been that of touching. With all the publicity about child sexual abuse and incest, I believe that my daughters may have extrapolated that lesbians/homosexuals molest children. One of my daughters, I believe, was turned off and upset by the full-frontal cuddling by one of my older lovers — it was over a year before she'd again let me hug her; once I understood what the problem was, as a mother I had to convince her that *maternal* touch/love was different from sexual touch/love. Similarly, I think that looking at bodies was a worry — will Mum want to perve on us? — although this need not have been a concern.

'*my son...unequivocally supported me*'
Credit; Parramatta Advertiser *1993*

My recent situation has involved an ongoing relationship with commitment to both a male and a female. As I approach the menopause, I see my future as being with a woman long-term, but perhaps with a few caring, platonic male and female friends.

My present girlfriend (whom I would like to be long-term) and I are now proud co-mothers of four cats and three children. We house-hop regularly as she lives just around the corner. She has admitted to me that she would like a child. I would of course be overjoyed to help her with this venture. She has taught me to love and care for cats and I, in turn, could help her with a child.

I do not feel overall that my bisexual lesbianism has been confusing for my children. In the long run I have, rather, broadened their options. Should they at some stage in the future wish to 'diversify', then they will have a firm base on which to build.

PAUL VAN REYK

Donor Dads
The sperm givers' view

I've read a lot about donor insemination from the perspective of the
women, most often lesbians, who've made this their child-bearing
choice. Over the years, having something of a reputation as a
donor, I've had the chance to put my views across, but I hadn't read
much from other gay male donors. I wondered what their perspective
was, what issues they saw. We talked about a lot of things; how we did
it; the set of relations to whom we donated; how for two of us it was as
donors that we had our first HIV test.

For each of us, this was the first chance we'd had to talk with other
gay men in a relatively safe way. As we talked, it seemed to me that
part of the reason for this was that donoring has raised complex
responses we find uncomfortable to talk about in the gay community.
Uncomfortable because they question our constructed gay identity,
particularly our political gay identity, and also open up the question of
the relationship of gay men and lesbians as partners in the donoring
process. It was particularly the conflict between patriarchy and
parenting that kept coming up.

Each of us comes from a background of gay liberation informed by
feminism. That framework means we see ourselves as involved in
combating patriarchy and its structures through the way we choose to
live our lives. Becoming donors was not only about supporting the
right of women to control their own reproduction, but also a challenge
to the construction of patriarchal relations through the heterosexual
family.

Steve's experience is common to us. "When I was first coming out I
moved into a leftie political scene. We were all talking about how we
didn't want to live the way our parents had done. The women didn't
want to raise children on their own. We talked about kids not having
parents, or being brought up in group households. I did it (donating)

as a political act. Out of the belief that we had the right to do anything we wanted. That being a lesbian didn't mean you couldn't have children, and that this was one way gay men could help."

For two of us, that overtly political dimension hasn't always been the case. We've each donated to a heterosexual couple where the male partner couldn't facilitate conception. But I'd hazard the guess that for most gay men who donate, the politics of what they are doing plays a large part in the decision.

Where that politics has led in many cases is to a practice of anonymous donations and multiple donors. None of my donations has been anonymous; I've always met the woman or couple. In all cases, the children know who their biological father is. The children know each other as brother and sister. They get together on birthdays. I've never reflected on the importance of that until I talked with the other donors.

They have all donated anonymously and now question that practice. Their concern is that anonymity is a political decision by adults which ends up denying children their right to a full identity.

Andy put it this way: "In the late '70s and early '80s we thought about children growing up in a non-patriarchal society, where hardly anyone lived with their mother or father anyway. But in another thirty years it won't be very different from what it is now. Much as we might have beliefs about this, the fact remains that children will become adults in a society where it matters who your father is, what your lineage is. That will force a whole range of questions for those children about their own identity, about who they are, about what they are made of."

"If the child wants to know and can't find out, then there's something they've lost a right to. The right to find out who their biological parent was."

Sean agrees. "There are enough children now who are adults trying to find their parents through adoption legislation. It's absurd to be replic-ating exactly the same situation."

I experienced something of that with my first son. The agreement had been that he would know about me and that we would see each other at a level of contact determined by his mothers. What we didn't count on was the level of contact he would want for himself. It intensified around the time he began going to school, but has now slackened. I think that's because for that time, proud as he was of having two mothers, he needed to establish his father to build a social identity. Now he needs that less.

For Peter, there is an added dimension to anonymity. He's donated three times, the first anonymously, the other two to women he's known before agreeing to be their donor. Both of the latter have been unsuccessful. This has been difficult for him. He spoke of the grieving he had gone through when coming out. The identity he constructed as a gay man was one which excluded the possibility of children. The option, he thought, just wasn't open. The failure of the two most recent donations has revived that grief. He now acknowledges that he would like to co-parent a child.

"I've identified my needs in the process and now that I know them I can't pretend that I don't have them. I can't just go ahead and do it as a political act and not acknowledge that it's something I need to do. I like the sort of man that I am and I like the sort of man a lot of the men I know are. I often think that it would be nice to share that with someone." When he thinks of a child, it is a boy he thinks of.

Because of this, Peter will not donate anonymously again. "One of the big unknowns is whether, if there was a child, I might one day have so much pain about that ... about having this child and not ever being able to contact it or have anything to do with it." If he donates at all again it will be with a woman with whom he has had a long-standing loose arrangement, where co-parenting at some level would be part of the contract.

Andy isn't about to do any more donating, and having a child was never a part of the decision to donate. But he, too, now recognises a need. "I could convince myself that I've deconstructed my need to have children. But I've become cynical about whether anyone really has the capacity to totally deconstruct any aspect of themselves that they don't want to have. At a certain level, the idea of there being someone who looks just like you and who is your friend but you have no parental relationship with, it's ... I catch myself out every now and then kind of feeling clucky. I suppose I've let myself indulge in those thoughts, or be honest with myself that I do have them."

Andy now has that need satisfied. There is a child which, though from multiple donors, he clearly recognises as his. He has made an agreement with the mother that should the child want to know, he will be identified as one of the potential fathers.

I don't recall any grieving over children foregone when coming out. I didn't donate out of a need for children. But I also can't deny that something in me is satisfied through them. I love seeing them together and tracing myself in them. I love watching them growing up and wondering how different from or similar to me they will be.

There have been unexpected changes for all of us through donoring, through putting a neat political theory into practice. The challenge becomes one of continuing the struggle against replicating patriarchal relations, while not denying our own needs or the needs of the children that we have been a party to parenting.

(The donors' names in this article are fictitious, at their request. This is to protect the identities both of the men who spoke openly to me of matters that were clearly difficult for them, and of the women to whom we have donated, and their children. If there is an incongruity between that and the content of the article, perhaps after all that is the point of the article.)

PAUL VAN REYK

Beyond Blood

What after all is there
beyond blood?
I can't be certain,
not now. Not yet.

Begin with the photograph.
Three of them by a backyard pool.
The photographer — Margaret? Kerrie?
has caught them sitting on the edge
ranged apparently by height
and so, by expectation, age.
(But it's a trick of the camera,
Jesse is surely smaller,
because younger, than Alexis?)
And how did they come to be
all wearing swimmers that shade
of pink?
It's a moment full of Bresson
revealing to an outside eye
more than intended.

Alexis holds up a foot,
cutting a figure
from synchronised swimming,
and scratches at something in her eye.
She's unaware of the shot.
(A moment later
she'll look up and know
she's missed something
and wonder what.)
Pity you miss her eyes,
Lascar black.

Jesse then, puppy rolls
at breast and hips

(how my body's flaccid forties
mirrors his)
tongue poking out, making a face
a grandmother who doesn't know him
would call cheeky.
He pushes into the frame
un-selfconscious still
before a camera,
though he knows its use
enough to mug.

Jay, smile a little forced,
shoulders hunched forward.
It's becoming important
to know this I, caught here
in the dilemma
of his rapidly maturing body.
Seeing the picture later
he'll feign embarrassment,
be fascinated
by the person he sees,
wonder whether he's okay.

Mary isn't in the picture,
so put beside this one
my snap on her tenth birthday,
her face half-shadowed
under an unruly purple felt hat.
A head and shoulders shot,
so you can't see
how gangly she is,
or her wonderfully big feet.
(She'd frown at this disclosure.)
She looks uncertain.
Her hair was bobbed yesterday
short for the first time in years.
It's a break with childhood
and perhaps she's not quite ready
for what the picture might define.
Or perhaps she's just tired
of another of dad's shots.

Brothers and sisters, these four,
from diverse patterns of parenting,
I the common biology.
It's this the photograph reveals.
The grouping, the pink cossies,
foreground blood.
But this is not t.v. soap,
not renaissance comedy
of brothers and sisters unknown
finding themselves grown lovers.
What, then, unsettles me?

Today, I hear a Premier rail
against the 'dangerous experiment'
of adoptive rights
for lesbians and gays. An experiment?
We've raised kids
for longer than it's taken
the heterorthodox family to emerge.

Still the barb catches.
We post-Stonewallers
have made of our lives
a social laboratory
experimenting with new forms
at each heterosexualised marker
of our development as social beings.
As with any trial of method or panacea,
this has always had a margin
for failure, a risk,
not always amenable
to assessment in advance.
Certainly I wondered
when entering these contracts
where it all might lead,
expected there would be times
when what we were doing,
never a coherent iconoclasm,
would be challenged.
None of us are quite
where we thought we would be.

But a margin for error
is different from danger.
And there is danger,
and I am afraid.

Blood has been no guarantee of safety
for the heterosexual family.
The toll of child abuse
and domestic violence mounts.
We ourselves know how thin
and cold blood runs
when we disclose desire;
know the violence of exile
and of fist;
know also the assault blood makes
reclaiming us as we lie dying.

If blood betrays or injures here
how will it protect us and ours,
in this experiment of family,
of clan, of tribe
or whatever anthropology they'll use
to limit this
consanguine fractal we live?
Not from the harm we may do,
(we will do no worse
and perhaps better
than the nominal control)
but that which may be done
by those to whom we are anathema —
the canting Premiers;
the collarless, colourless clerics;
the legislators, bellies full
of apples gone sour;
god and state shoring up
their dream of home
sliding into slum.

Mary is ten, Jay nearly so,
as I was when brought here
to a country foreign as expected
in geography and climate,

but whose lived frame I,
child of Sri Lankan burghers,
and so raised white,
assumed would fit.
Each year brought proof
that I was alien.
Hard, the distance
this country placed
between me and me
and between me and blood.
So they stand now
at the border of a country
not of new geographies
but relationships
they assume are theirs,
but from which they will with time
discover themselves, too, alien.
They have already faced
the hate and hurt of race.
How I've wished
I could have spared them this,
not self-hating of race,
but that something I have given
should be the cause of pain.
I cannot bear we should endure
the severing and suturing,
the finding out by others
of the subversive acts
of their conception and nurturing.

But if not blood
then what?

I have two more pictures.
In the first, three brothers
in white shirts and khaki shorts
stand shoulder to shoulder
before a hedge. The light
confirms it is another country.
They don't touch.
But something in the way
each looks unforced into the camera,

or perhaps it is the phalanx
they make between the camera
and their home behind the hedge,
assures you these three
together will come through
the years ahead.
Here they are now, gathered
with wives, partners, kids,
spilling down the backyard steps
of their parents' home,
a looser confederation
but bearing out the promise.

It's taken me thirty years
to traverse to a homecoming
still tentative
and incomplete (a grandmother
turns the pages of an album
that shows only a grand-daughter),
but happily not too late.
So, not without equivocation,
I have hope in blood,
that there will yet be
a photograph, frame overcrowded
with the chaos
of what it is we have produced,
and what these four
will produce in turn,
the filigrees of their fractal lives,
whole and held.

GARY DUNNE

Happy little vegemites

I'm as civic-minded as the next person. I take note of what's happening in the big wide world and like to do my bit to help when I can. Initially, the International Year of the Family had me stumped. I've never been clear about this Western version of Chinese astrology. Each year they come up with a group for us to patronise and feel guilty about. Sometimes some good comes out of it, such as the Mabo legislation, but generally it's just a pervasive theme. Exactly how you're meant to get involved is far from obvious.

By late January in 1994, it seemed that the most I'd be contributing to IYF would be an angry reaction to certain Nationals and fundamentalist right-wingers who were taking pot shots, Dan Quayle style, at any form of family that didn't have a biological father at work and a biological mother in the kitchen. To quote Louise Wakeling, it's the quality of the nurturing, not the number, sex or sexuality of the parent/s that is the issue. The fifties was a fabulous decade for fashion and film, but it finished over thirty years ago. Someone had to tell the Nationals this and, given their thickness, it might have taken all year.

Then out of the blue, I was contacted by a lesbian couple, friends of friends, asking if I'd be willing to donate some sperm to start their family. To cut a long story short, I said yes. It wouldn't be a new experience for me. I gave generously during the pre-AIDS lesbian baby boom.

There are a number of fine books and a very efficient grape-vine available for dykes who wish to become pregnant with a minimum of unpleasantness. Unfortunately, there is very little in print for gay men considering donating to the process.

In the March '94 issue of *Burn* I wrote about sperm donating, calling my most recent experiences a positive contribution to the International Year of the Family. The considerable volume of feedback to that column was quite unexpected. There were many gay men who were undecided or unwilling to donate and wanted to discuss the issues in greater depth. I also heard from lesbians who were having problems finding a donor. Was I willing or did I know of anyone?

Had *Burn* continued I would have written about subsequent conversations I had with a wide variety of gay men. A surprising number suffered from what I can only call a genetic inferiority complex. A family history of heart disease, colour blindness or asthma was enough for them to say 'no' to dabbling in the gene pool. While I'd understand not wanting some genetic bits and pieces, such as Huntington's chorea, being handed on to the next generation, I was concerned about the implications of what these men were actually saying. The reality is that no one's perfect. I was talking about creating families, not eugenics or a master race. The same genes hadn't stopped their parents, and in most cases their siblings, from unrestrained breeding.

The other issue of interest was the cultural, emotional and legal consequences of 'fathering' a child in a patriarchal society. While even a totally anonymous donation requires consideration, if you and the child will know each other the implications are greater.

Firstly, there's the legal angle. Can this person make a claim on your estate? Should your name be on the birth certificate? If so, what are your legal responsibilities? I was advised that unless it was agreed that I'd be closely involved, it would probably be better to leave my name off the certificate. As yet there have been no test cases concerning sperm donors, so the situation remains legally unclear.

Then there are the cultural and emotional aspects. Over-simplified, the question is, do you tell your parents they've become grandparents? Whatever your answer, the person you have to justify it to is yourself.

It comes down to whether you see being a parent as an ownership of biological off-spring (the 'my progeny, my property' theory) or as simply an acceptance of the ongoing full-time responsibility of raising a child ('the brat stops here' theory).

I tend strongly towards the second view, seeing parenthood as an undervalued essential social role. Foster and adopting parents are no different from biological parents; all deserve the same gold medals as far as I'm concerned.

Along with that view, I also believe it's important for kids to have a variety of significant adults around during their upbringing. The old extended family had qualities the current nuclear family often lacks; aunties, uncles, cousins and grandparents with whom kids have an ongoing close relationship. As with parenthood, I believe it's the role these people play in kids' lives, not their biological similarities, that is important.

I've been a (non-related) member of a couple of extended families for over twenty years. Being an uncle is a role that starts with nappies and baby-sitting, proceeds through school concerts, holidays together, Easter shows, movies, coffee lounges and bars, culminating in drunken speeches at 21sts, weddings or the departure lounge as they set off to explore the wider world.

During the eighties I spent three months playing responsible adult to three feral adolescents (10, 14 and 15) whose parents were off doing the grand tour of Europe. My first, and probably only, attempt at full-time parenting was a rare experience for all four of us. We organised the funeral of one of their grandparents and attended Casualty several times. There were a multitude of minor disasters, most of which we had cleaned up in time for the return of the parents (except for the breakages that occurred during the teens and queens dinner party, an event that most of the forty or so participants still recall with bemused horror).

I recall demanding instant attention at the Children's Hospital with a level of justified assertion that I've never displayed before or since. ("Auntie Gaz went all bolshie and we got seen straight away," was a sibling's verdict.)

My point is that the urge to care for kids is innate, and the kids don't have to be fruit of the loins for that kind of mutual adoption to occur. Proximity and a similar sense of humour are probably all that's necessary to spark the relationship, and it can be as close or as distant as you want it to be.

As someone with no urge to take on parenting as a permanent position, I'm quite happy being an uncle. I doubt if I'd be any more protective or loving towards a child I'm related to than I've been with my nieces and nephews.

To date, I haven't really had the chance to find out. I donated for two women in the early eighties. In the first situation I was one of a number of donors and am not the biological father of the child. In the second situation, handled through a mutual friend, I donated without knowing the mother at all. The mother and her partner were worried about a biological father's potential claim on their child so wanted the situation, from my point of view, to be anonymous. They know who I am, however, and our agreement back then was that the child had the right to know too. Being honest, I've not really thought much about it since then, but guess I'd cope with a knock on the door, if it ever happens.

My most recent donation on Mardi Gras '94 Fair Day, worked first time, and I'm curious about how I'll feel about this child. (At the time of writing, the mother is five months pregnant and doing well.) My arrangement with the mothers is that we'll keep in touch and see what kind of relationship the kid wants, the major determining factor which it's not possible to predict or plan in advance.

Within an extended family framework, a relationship between donor father and child can be enriching for both. Certainly that's the case in a number of families started in the early '80s. Elsewhere in this book are the stories of Paul and Jay, a relationship no one, least of all the mothers and the donor, predicted. Seeing how their relationship has developed over the past decade had a major influence on my most recent discussions about donating.

Another story in this anthology deals with anonymous deposits in sperm banks. What follows are some practical observations for (gay) men thinking about donating for (lesbian) friends.

It begins with blood tests. HIV is the obvious one, but it seems to me that every time I get tested, there are more things to be tested for. There used to be only two kinds of hepatitis, now there are at least four. The second HIV test is three months after the first, allowing plenty of time for thinking through the implications of donating and for chatting with the prospective parent/s.

Assuming you're all negative, it's time to work through the finer details. The first question is: How involved do you want to be? They'll have their own expectations. Options vary from not at all to co-parenting, with most gay donors I know opting for a position in between, a version of the uncle role I mentioned earlier.

Once that's resolved, the conversation will turn to their need to have some idea of what they're getting in a genetic sense. Your biological family histories, from poor eyesight to the fact that you are about as cute as your genetic line gets, are all relevant. Family photos, what relatives have died of, diseases, abilities and personalities all become significant.

The donations themselves should be the easy bit. A quick wank into a Vegemite jar on the right days each month and Grace is your uncle. There are a few points for novices, however. Firstly, don't expect too much. Those Californian and French fillums have a lot to answer for. The average male does not produce as much semen as the average porn star. (I don't know why.) In fact, looking at the small volume in the bottom of your Vegemite jar can be quite sobering. Not coming for a few days beforehand and taking as long as possible over the production process increases it a bit, but expect to be at least slightly bemused.

Location is the other problem. Given my own erotic history, I didn't expect I'd encounter any difficulty in producing sperm in an unfamiliar or unusual environment. Life, however, wasn't meant to be easy in a lesbian bathroom. Request the wet knickers be removed from the curtain rails beforehand and don't ponder the patriarchy or watch yourself in the mirror, if you're given to giggling. You'll only have to start all over again. Bring some porn or a friend, if either is likely to be of assistance.

My own experience is that it's easiest to do it yourself at home and let the non-biological mother collect the Vegemite jar and take it back to their place. As freshness is important, this only works if you live near each other.

The rest is up to Mother Nature who, thankfully, unlike those in charge of the commercial sperm banks, is a woman who doesn't discriminate.

The only other question I've been asked about sperm donating is: what's in it for the donor, or more simply, why do it? As a gay man I'd have to say that it's life-affirming in an era characterised by loss. As a political coalitionist and strong supporter of lesbian rights, I'd say it's a gift, a bond of trust between significant friends.

Postscript: In November '94 Madeleine was born. Having written about and discussed the topic in abstract terms for the past nine months, it was a kind of shock to all of us to realise that what we had been talking about was this unique tiny person. Holding her in my arms, filled with protective tenderness, I was relieved on two accounts. Firstly, I didn't have an overwhelming urge to hand out phallic symbols, and secondly, she hadn't inherited a Dunne nose. I'm looking forward to getting to know her.

STEPHEN DUNNE

I was a closet Queer sperm donor

Ican't be certain, but apparently I have at least two children, and possibly more. I don't know where they are or how they are faring — I don't even know their names or gender. I know I have at least two because the nicer nurse at the clinic told me, even though she wasn't supposed to. All I really know is that, in about two decades, it is possible a couple of tall, myopic and slightly awkward kids (who, despite my best hopes, probably won't be queer) will turn up on my doorstep/gutter, gaze at my ravaged face in wonder and say, "Hi. You're my genetic father," or words to that effect.

It was via a small advertisement in *Newswit,* the student newspaper of the University of Technology Sydney, that I entered the shadowy world of the sperm donor. I don't know if the legendary phallic tower of that institution provided an unconscious reason for the ad appearing there. I didn't care about such subtleties then — I was only interested in the fine print: 'Expenses Paid ($20)'.

To put it into context, I was the then-obligatory Starving Arts Student living in a multi-coloured slum in the wrong end of Surry Hills. You know the type — lentils, cask wine, drugs when the Austudy came through, and anti-capitalist posturing in inverse proportion to the amount of ready cash on hand.

The idea of being paid $20 a time to jerk off into a jar held much financial appeal. I rang the clinic and was asked in for a medical. I was also told that my sperm count and sperm 'motility' (how good the little pinheads are at thrashing their tails) would be measured. In order to ensure a bumper crop, I was told to abstain from any form of ejaculation for a week. (A week is a *very* long time for a twenty year old with a popular beat five minutes walk from home).

When I arrived, a mass of suppurating hormones ready to squirt at the slightest stimulus, I was handed a specimen jar and taken upstairs to 'the room'. This room was to be a small (but financially rewarding) part of my erotic life for the next three years. It was small, smaller than the second bedroom of a '70s flat. It had a bed (single of course), with a bedside table containing tissues, KY and a pile of black label *Penthouse*. The walls were covered in garish arty porn posters (a Conette the fem Barbarian, a woman licking a banana etc), all exclusively heterosexual. 'The Room' was also thankfully air conditioned.

The first time was easy, though I soon encountered the major difficulty of sperm donation — aim. Speaking personally, at the critical moment generally the last thing I am interested in is holding a little plastic jar over the end of my dick to catch the allegedly precious fluid. My hands would much rather be sliding, rubbing and tweaking. However, you had to catch the lot — there was nothing more embarrassing than providing a small sample, appearing inadequate because half of it shot onto your stomach (though I became very adept at scraping renegade semen off parts of my body and putting it back in the jar). Regardless, the enormous amount I learnt about muscle control at the point of orgasm during those years has been useful for my erotic technique, especially in tricky group situations, ever since.

On that first day, I got it all in and, trying not to pant too noticeably, walked down the stairs clutching my jar of warm cum. I smiled at the secretary (after all, it's not as if there's anything embarrassing about wandering around an Eastern Suburbs medical complex carrying your own ejaculate), deposited the jar where I was told to and picked up my first $20. I was then hustled off for my medical.

They paid a lot of attention to the plumbing — "Cough!" Once the good doctor realised my dick appeared to work and my balls were lump free, we got onto the real reason for the medical — the questions.

The first half was primitive eugenics, designed to determine if I was of good breeding stock (while there's more than a touch of the Naziesque in this idea, I should point out that the most sought after donors at this clinic were men of South East Asian and Chinese descent). Then, questions about family medical history — cancer, schizophrenia, heart disease and all the other so-called 'inheritable' illnesses.

Next, we moved onto the more interesting questions.

"Have you had any form of sex with men since 1980?"

"No," I lied.

"Have you ever used intravenous drugs?"

"No," I said — I'd certainly done the substances, but not in the arm due to needle-phobia.

"Have you had a blood transfusion or taken blood products since 1980?"

"No," I said, correctly assuming that black pudding didn't count.

(The point of this was not clear until much later — it seemed strange given that I was tested for HIV, hep, syphilis and gonorrhoea every three months. For any of my frozen sperm to be released, I had to have two consecutive clear tests, so possible HIV transmission wasn't the worry. What they were trying to do was to weed out any honest queers. After all, the middle-class hets who were to pay handsomely for my genetic pattern didn't want — gasp — fag sperm in their applicator syringes.)

Next came eugenics part two — what did I get in my HSC? What was I studying now? Could I play any musical instruments? What sports did I like? On the unlikely assumption that such abilities and proclivities were inherited rather than environmental, the middle-class families who were after a sperm bank wanted to ensure the best possible genetic chance for their treasured offspring.

My details were encoded onto a card, which went into a file, sort of like a human stud book. Prospective customers would then flick through the cards, looking for the physical and intellectual qualities they desired in their kids. (According to the nice nurse, who gossiped, I was quite popular on account of being tall, being able to play the piano and studying in the 'arts'. Presumably, if I'd possessed blue eyes, I could have gone into the sperm-manufacture business full time.)

All donors were only ever known by a two-letter code. Mine was XY, and every time I charged into that room to box the jesuit for cash, there was some slight feeling that, due to my chromosomal code-name, I was meant to be typical of my gender.

Over three years I regularly made the trip to the clinic, grabbed my little jar from the receptionist and went upstairs to 'spend', as the Victorians would have said. The most interesting moments occurred when the room was already 'occupied', and I had to wait. The sight of a cute lad, extremely embarrassed, leaving the jerkoff room clutching his own cum while I waited my turn was particularly edifying. I soon learnt an elaborate code of behaviour with my fellow donors — a nod, a wave, a 'hey, isn't this bizarre' kind of smile.

Despite often wishing that some of my fellow donors would join me in a produce extraction session (a more efficient use of time after all), it never happened. And, for all those nervous donor-receptive families out there, I was by no means the only queer sperm donor. In fact, it was usually a case of 'hunt the het'. If the gay gene theory is true, my brothers and I have done a sterling job in swelling our ranks of tomorrow.

Our more unreconstructed politicians, especially the ones in moleskins and those silly hats, tend to talk about us having kids as something that is relevant to the area of public policy, and that 'Something Should Be

Done'. This is silly in itself — what exactly do they plan? Ban all turkey basters, syringes and plungers? Even then, we could just close our eyes and actually fuck. But, I can now reveal that the International Homosexual Conspiracy has been targeting IVF programs for years. We're out there, madly jerking into jars, deliberately spreading that mythical gay gene and turning your lovely proto-het children into Mauve Mafia Cuckoos.

Over time, the sheer familiarity of the wanking cell led to a certain boredom. Getting all hot and bothered over the (supplied) copies of *Penthouse* was never likely, even when reading the letters and dizzily imagining myself in the female position ("He was so big, and as he slid into me, I knew Chad was the man of my dreams . . ."). In time, I started to bring my own porn and even, on special occasions, some toys. My other technique revolved around the fact that the suburb where the clinic was located had (and still has) a very stylish beat. Often, I'd go there, engage in as-close-to-sex-as-I-could-get-without-actually-doing-it, in order to reach a level of undeniable stimulation, rush down the road with my bag covering my hard-on, grab the jar and go for it. Occasionally, I got too carried away in the beat, and had to go home more satisfied, but *sans* the $20.

I lasted for over three years — three years of buses to the clinics, wanking and a blood test every three months. As I said, the nice gossipy nurse told me that two of my impregnations had been successful, so I suppose I can assume that, barring pre-natal accidents, I have at least two genetic kiddies out there.

It's odd — if, as a few heterosexual geneticists believe, our basic function in life is to pass on our genetic material, then the wonders of science (along with the drudges of studentry) have conspired to allow me to surpass my supposed non-reproductive bent, being queer and all. In this world of selfish genes, I can now happily die, having performed my duty to the species. Even though, in crude evolutionary terms, I probably wasn't meant to.

It's a vaguely comforting thought, to know you have children. It's even more comforting to be in the rare situation of knowing you have them without them having the slightest effect on your life. All the soft glow of fatherhood, with no responsibility. On the other hand, it's quite pleasant to imagine being a proper sperm donor, playing Uncle Arthur for a couple of dykes, turning up once every two months to pat some tyke on the head and spoil it rotten. Unfortunately, I'm still looking for a lesbian who'll pay me $20 an attempt. After all, I was a professional — there are standards to maintain, and I would hate anyone to think I was scabbing.

PEARLIE McNEILL

Here comes the groom

This article has been written with the approval and support of Marie McShea and Meg Coulson. All other names used are fictitious.

England 1990. It was the scene outside the church that bothered me the most. I lay awake worrying about it, night after night. Who would line up alongside Catherine and Chris when the photographer called for the happy couple's parents? Would my ex-husband and his wife (my ex-best friend) dare to take centre stage, despite not having had anything to do with Chris for almost nine years? How would Catherine's family and friends respond when I stepped forward, flanked by my partner Meg and my ex-lover Marie? I was uncompromising in my expectations. I wanted Meg and Marie to stand alongside me, to be accepted for who they were.

Back in 1978 Marie and I had begun a relationship. Chris had been eleven years old then and Trystan thirteen. We became a family of five when Marie gave birth to Susannah in 1981. I had no doubts whatsoever that Marie had earned the right to be acknowledged as Chris's parent. Meg, too, had contributed a great deal. She had been (and still is) my partner since 1986 and though *all* our lives continued to change in various ways around that time, the commitment to young people continued and even widened, to include four children from Lancaster whom Meg had known and helped care for since their early childhood.

In my late night fantasy Catherine and Chris walked out of the church into dappled sunshine (fingers crossed about the weather) smiling for the camera, obligingly, self-consciously. But my mind came to a whizz-bang halt just when the crucial moment arrived. I simply couldn't move the scene along, couldn't envisage how we three women would handle the situation. I didn't realise at first how stunned I really was. I felt trapped, stuck in a tiny groove, going over the same things again and again. It was all so unexpected. The thought that one of my sons might choose to marry had never occurred to me. Any wedding would have been a challenge, but to attend this one under these circumstances, as mother of the groom?

I kept replaying a conversation Chris and I had had late in December 1989, days before I left for a four months' working holiday in Australia. He'd talked briefly about his relationship with Catherine, insisting there was no suggestion of them living together. Besides, Catherine was only eighteen, he'd added, and neither of them was ready for such a big step.

We had a deal, he and I. As long as the commitment between him and Catherine was low-key and mostly social, I'd accept his decision NOT to reveal that his mother was a lesbian. If their relationship deepened, became more permanent, he'd be expected to keep his promise to tell all, to Catherine and to her parents, at the earliest, most opportune, moment.

In February, a letter arrived at Trystan's Sydney address. We'd set up this arrangement because I was moving around a lot. Excited and impatient, I asked Trystan to read it over the phone.

"If only I could tell you this face to face instead of in a letter ..."

Trystan struggled to read the letter and I began to cry.

Catherine was pregnant. They'd both assumed that when the doctor had prescribed the contraceptive pill, to help regulate Catherine's periods, it would also work as a contraceptive. The baby was due late August. Catherine's parents were not in favour of abortion. The wedding was planned for June, soon after my arrival back in England.

From the moment that letter arrived I was in turmoil. The phone calls I had with Chris over the next few days were strained and almost unbearable. His replies to my questions were constantly interrupted and overshadowed by comments from Catherine's mother. At the end of each five minute call Agnes would take over, conveying updated information about a long list of arrangements and winding up with a plea that I simply relax and enjoy myself 'over there', and come back full of anticipation for a wonderful wedding day. Agnes assured me she would see to everything.

My trip to Australia had been planned for a long time. There were four of us travelling together; Marie, Susannah, Meg and me. I would not have flown back to England even if I could have afforded the fare. I had commitments and wouldn't have chosen otherwise, but I was sorely aware that Chris and Catherine had no one, apart from her family, to talk to. The next letter made clear that Chris had explained *everything* to Catherine and had also told her parents and brother Clive. He made no comment as to how this news was received.

Chris's decision to keep others from knowing too soon about my lesbianism had not developed, as you might think, from a tendency to homophobia on his part, but was linked directly to his own experience of discrimination because of *other* people's homophobic responses to me.

When the boys started school in the early 1970s I was married and living in the western suburbs. I had a fear then that public high school education, particularly in the west, would be more like entering a factory than a school. As parents, Peter and I felt we were thinking ahead when we chose to send the boys to a nearby Catholic school. There was nothing remarkable or special about the school. It was small, class numbers were low, and we felt these benefits more than justified the effort needed to pay the fees each term.

When my marriage broke up I moved to an inner-city area, renting a flat in a large house. The house was owned by a feminist and occupied by women. The boys were able to transfer to a Catholic school in Lewisham. In his last year of primary school a year later, Chris mentioned to his lay teacher that his mother's partner was a woman. I guessed this information had been passed around a bit, yet no one seemed bothered. One male teacher, newly arrived from the bush in 1980, visited the boys at home, met Marie and me, and came back several times. Had we given him half a chance, I have no doubt he would happily have moved in as an honorary third son.

Things continued on much as before, that is, until Brother John took over as school principal, and decided that Trystan was unruly and disruptive. It is true that Trystan had been ticked off by a prefect for carving entwined initials, his and a girlfriend's, into the back of a bus-stop seat. Further incriminating evidence came when one of the senior brothers spotted him in a shopping centre late one Thursday afternoon, wearing a jeans jacket with the sleeves cut out. Then came a week-end when he left his school shoes behind at his father's place. I insisted Monday morning that sneakers were a better option than taking a day off. During assembly Brother John noted the offending footwear. Trystan was immediately escorted into his office by two prefects. After a lengthy dressing down about unacceptable behaviour, Brother John then expressed his views about lesbians, making it plain to Trystan that his mother was despicable, disgraceful, disgusting, as well as being 'a sinful, immoral woman both in the eyes of God and in the eyes of Man'.

The boys' Catholic school education ended that day. I quickly understood, after several distressing phone calls, that I couldn't take on the Catholic Church, unwilling as I was to allow further insult to my sons and with no promise of a positive outcome. I cannot say though, even now, that I regret sending them to Catholic schools. We know, don't we, that prejudice and bigotry exist across a broad spectrum. The conclusions that arose from our experience centred only around Brother John.

Trystan and Chris were soon enrolled at the local high school, and everything was done to help them make the adjustment as smoothly as possible. Unexpectedly, Peter called by the next week to announce he was seeking a divorce. His plan was to marry Rita as soon as he was free. Only a few days earlier I learned they'd been seeing each other for several months. She hadn't chosen to tell me, but he had. Perhaps she would have felt uncomfortable? Embarrassed? Not Peter, he'd been in a mood to boast. Since leaving the marriage, I'd avoided the subject of divorce, fearing, with some justification, that he would make an issue of my lifestyle in court. He'd threatened to insist on sole custody, and I had been reluctant to take on a battle I could so easily lose. Ironically, his tactics changed overnight, a convenient adjustment to his new situation. The threat to me was dropped, replaced by the intention to abandon his children. And here he stood, hèavy with pronouncements. I would not have minded that so much had he not insisted that Trystan and Chris hear every single word. He had given up too many years already for the sake of the boys, he declared, it was time he had a life of his own. In future he wanted only occasional contact with his sons. They were almost grown up now.

They simply had to understand that he'd had enough. Handing me a sheaf of papers, he headed for the door.

This rejection, following so soon after the episode with Brother John, was to have a devastating effect on both Trystan and Chris, though nothing they said or did that night gave any clue as to what lay ahead.

The sequence of events over the next six months remains hazy in my mind. Was Marie pregnant when the boys left St Thomas's? When did the letter arrive informing us that Trystan was not attending school? Was that before or after we heard that Chris had slipped from being a cheerful boy, near the top of his class, to a depressed youngster in need of remedial reading lessons?

I clearly remember my see-sawing responses to Trystan's imploding fury. It was a bitter blow when he left home, not yet sixteen, only weeks before Susannah was born, and, promptly set about blaming my lesbianism for everything untoward that had ever happened to him. It was the school counsellor who found him a place in a young person's refuge at Paddington. In town one day Trystan approached me. I drew back, wondering how the hell this stranger knew my name. The much-admired, auburn hair had been dyed, matching perfectly the unfamiliar clothes — black jeans, shirt, leather waistcoat and skinny pointed boots that looked at least three sizes too big. If he hadn't spoken I would have passed him by. He did come home to see the baby, but it was to be another five years before we could have a peaceful conversation again.

Meanwhile, Chris's self-confidence was waning and he began describing himself as stupid. He was communicative still, but it was obvious he was confused and unhappy. He cheered up the night Susannah was born, expressing excitement and responsible concern when the midwife gave him small tasks to do, making a point of repeating her instructions to be sure he understood. He loved Susannah from the very first moment and was keen to be involved with caring for her. Susannah has always been a cherished, much-wanted baby, but the continuous swirl of emotions was inevitably exhausting, and affected each of us in different ways.

The divorce case went through without too much hassle and Peter and Rita were married in due course. Trystan and Chris heard all about the wedding several months later. They never did ask why they hadn't been invited. For a long time I walked around with this odd feeling that someone close to me had died. Rita had been my friend from the very day we'd moved into the same street. We had planned the birth of two of our children to coincide and almost succeeded. Chris is three months younger than Rita's third child, also a boy. Abandoned by her own husband, she had been so scathing about mine. What had changed her mind, I wondered? No way was I going to ask, better simply to withdraw. Chris was also hurting. I could tell he felt replaced in his father's affections by Rita's younger son, that same boy only three months older than himself.

My anger was persistent and purposeful. Okay, I'd lost one son, but damned if I was going to give the other one up without a fight. I had to do something, but what?

The small business Marie and I had set up in 1979 involved the publication of a few titles, running a bookshop and making infrequent selling trips in a campervan, up and down the east coast, between Brisbane and Melbourne. Things were not going well. The bookshop was not in a good position and we were beginning to lose money, hand over fist. Reluctantly, we agreed it was time to quit. We came up with the idea of selling the house, buying a cheaper one and travelling overseas with the surplus from the sale. We planned to be away from Australia for a year. This decision proved to be a good one for Chris. Removed from the situation with his father, he flourished in rural Devon. This time, we kept our lifestyle strictly private for the sake of the children. Chris's attitude to schoolwork improved only slightly, but he did take a keen interest in sport. In his last year he won the school's Citizenship Award, which was no mean feat for a colonial boy in an English school. The following year Marie decided to study Homoeopathy, a four year course, and I settled down to write and to teach Creative Writing. Susannah, always a happy child, took to water like a duck, proving herself to be a good swimmer quite early on. Our twelve month stay stretched, remarkably, to thirteen years.

But, in the hectic weeks before we left for England, a grim struggle ensued between us and a tabloid newspaper. In recent years I had written a few pieces for *Forum (Australia)* during the time Bettina Arndt was editor. At my suggestion, Marie wrote an article about alternative conception, intending to make the information, and what we'd learned from the experience, accessible to other women. Not only did Bettina Arndt like the article, she wanted to use it for the launch issue of a new magazine. We were 'out' lesbians, so Marie used her own name. When the magazine hit the streets, Marie's article was picked up by this Sunday newspaper and we suddenly found ourselves at the centre of an explosive situation. In negotiation with the editor my intention was to keep our names out of the limelight. He had already made it quite clear the story was going to run, whether we liked it or not. It seemed our names *could* be kept out of it, if in return, we would agree to hand over the photograph I'd taken to accompany the article. This photograph showed mother and baby in profile, foreheads touching. It could have been almost ANY mother and baby and I doubted whether anyone would have recognised Marie or Susannah so I agreed, relieved to have got off so lightly.

The story appeared the Sunday before we left, November 1981. Not satisfied with the snapshot as it was, the newspaper decided to whip up a more scandalous image and ran it on the front page, with two oblong blacked out sections over the eyes (including Susannah's) and a caption alongside that read: LESBIAN MUM'S AMAZING CONFESSION ... see Page 2.

Page two made no reference to Marie's article or the new magazine, and gave the impression that the reporter had unearthed this depraved couple and their fearful secret all on his own. The Rev. Fred Nile was quoted as saying we were an 'abomination and a grievous sin.' We did manage to laugh about that one and could never quite work out which of us was which.

Susannah was now five months old. Chris was fourteen. Trystan had recently turned sixteen. At the airport he told us not to worry, he would be alright. We'd asked him repeatedly to come, but he had other plans. As I hugged him goodbye I felt both concern and relief. Perhaps he shared my ambivalence? Days later he helped burgle a flat. Too scared to do much, he acted as lookout whilst two of his mates did the business inside. The next day, when the two went back for a second go, the police just happened to be dusting the place for fingerprints. Trystan was picked up within the hour. He was placed on probation for eighteen months, but was so scared at being in trouble with the law, you could almost say it was a good thing. In 1985 he was badly burned in an accident and I flew back to Australia in a mad panic. For the second time I failed to recognise my son. This time his hair was a different kind of black, standing up in tufts at the back, singed to a mere stubble in front. His skin was blackened too, shaped in ugly ridges, more a grotesque mask than a human face.

"No," I said firmly to the nurse, "that's not my son." I heard the sob as I moved away. Peering closer I noticed a tear leak out of one eye. "Trystan?" I asked, trying to contain my horror.

It was a slow and painful recovery for Trystan and he still bears traces of the scars on his face and both arms, but it was the start of a new dialogue between us. Of course, Trystan couldn't talk at first but he did manage to scrawl a few words onto a paper pad. The last time I saw him in the hospital, he was well enough to be wheeled around in a special chair. He'd undergone two operations, to graft skin from his thighs onto both arms, and was optimistic he'd be playing his guitar in another few months. His life had lacked direction these last four years. Would the accident effect a change in how he faced the future? We agreed he'd had a lucky escape and that something as traumatic as this required him to think carefully about what was happening in his life. As time has passed, it is evident that the accident marked a turning point in Trystan's understanding of himself, his childhood and the people in his life.

Now, almost five years to the day since Trystan's accident, Chris was getting married. There were so many things to think about, to worry about, but despite my feelings I would, in the end, accept the choice Chris was making, even if as I suspected the choice had not been made actively by either him or Catherine. Rediscovering my sense of humour, I concentrated on practical things. What to wear, for instance? How to get around the parochial thinking of a small Devon village? What exactly are mothers-in-law supposed to wear for such occasions? It soon became a joke among my friends, and some of the suggestions were hilarious.

Back in England a Danish lesbian friend offered to make me a three piece suit, in a shade of blue, acceptable, we thought, for a non-frilly female to choose for a wedding. The Danish touch was an imported method for using material with a special adhesive to create picture patterns. I chose satin, the same blue as the suit. The back of the jacket featured a tree with outstretched branches. Here and there small birds nestled among the leaves in various groupings. Machined embroidery held the whole thing in place. We intended the design to work like a code for those in the know, and managed to include a triangle on the waistcoat. The trousers were comfortable and wrinkle-free and I had previously bought a cream silk shirt that would go quite well. Shoes were the biggest challenge. Reluctantly, I bought white sling-backs with a small heel, beseeching Sappho (and anyone else I could think of) to allow me this one small concession. The hat was a riot. I was sure it had to be fate when I saw it in a department store. The blue was perfect, and I loved the solitary feather sticking out at a jaunty angle. By the time I got to wear it, I was convinced I looked like Marjorie Maine in one of those old films about Ma and Pa Kettle down on the farm.

When the day finally arrived I was spoiling for a fight. Agnes was proving hard to pin down when it came to information about how the head table was to be arranged. Rita and Peter had arrived the night before and were staying in a bed-and-breakfast establishment down the road. I had a nasty suspicion that Agnes was deliberately avoiding me, hoping that by the time I arrived at the reception venue, I'd agree, rather than cause a scene, to sit where I was told. Did she intend to shove me off to the side in favour of Rita and Peter?

The groom was resplendent in his hired morning suit. We three women and the Best Man, an old friend from Chris's schooldays, walked with him down to the church, cracking jokes, pretending not to notice how nervous he was.

Down the aisle came the bridesmaids in long, lolly pink dresses, all four of them resembling steps and stairs versions of Little Bo Peep. Susannah's upward swept hairdo, caught on top with fake flowers and tulle trim, was a bit sophisticated for a ten year old, but her sparkling eyes and happy grin softened the impact. She gave us a little wave as she walked by. Catherine swept by in a cleverly-styled white dress that fitted firmly at the bustline but became loose and flowing the nearer it got to the floor. What a relief it was to watch the antics of the youngest brides-maid, a chubby two year old, whose laughter and giggles made such a welcome contrast to the thunder and brimstone sentiments of the vicar. Four bell-ringers pulled and heaved on thick, jute ropes as we all piled out of the church. The photographer, a local man, had to be reminded the groom had a family at all.

The reception venue was within walking distance, down the bottom of a steep hill. Catherine and Chris were already positioned at the door, greeting guests, when we arrived. Agnes and Bill could be seen hurrying from table to table, saying their hullos and showing people where to sit. Meg and I made a beeline for the head table and sure enough, there was my name on a placecard, positioned to one side of the head table. We looked in vain for Meg's name. Before I had time to check where Rita and Peter were to sit, I glanced up and saw Agnes advancing towards me. If I was going to do something it had to be now. I plopped myself down in the nearest seat. Was I next to the groom or was it the bride? Did it matter? Did I care? The main thing was that I'd scored my seat of honour and that was that. Seconds before Agnes reached me I spotted her handbag. It was navy blue and looked like a large envelope. It had been placed between the knife and fork directly in front of me. Then I saw her name. I hadn't planned this but here I was, sitting in the very place Agnes had chosen for herself.

I looked up in time to catch the uncertainty in her eyes. Smiling at me as though we were the closest of friends, she indicated my allotted place at the end of the table. I didn't hear her words but knew instantly she was going to pretend I had mistakenly sat in the wrong place. I looked her full in the face before opening my mouth.

"I have a right to be here, Agnes, and this is where I'm staying."

I kept my voice low but there was no doubt I meant every word I said. What she didn't know was how badly my legs were shaking and how grateful I was to have Meg standing nearby. Agnes stood stock still, unsure what to do next. I held her handbag in my grasp, waiting for her to take it. She snatched it away and walked hurriedly to the far side of the table where her son Clive was standing with his girlfriend. It didn't require much imagination to guess what was being said. I watched and waited. When Clive looked over and shot me a filthy look, I deliberately misinterpreted him. Picking up a glass of wine I raised it in his direction as though making a toast.

And so it was that Agnes sat at the side table on her daughter's wedding day, whilst I sat next to the groom. Bill was Master of Ceremonies, so it was fitting that he sit next to Catherine. Peter was given the seat I'd rejected and Rita got to sit with Meg and Marie at the long table nearby. I doubt that anyone but those involved realised there'd been a showdown at high noon. I've often wondered if even Chris and Catherine ever knew what really happened.

Standing up to Agnes was not simply an act of assertion. Attitudes are slow to change, and those of us who live our lives in alternative ways, who rear our children in alternative ways, have to fight persistently and with vigour for recognition and respect from the wider world, and there'll be times when we feel equal to that struggle and many times when we won't. Our gains are not usually measured in great triumphs, but in brief moments that we learn to hug tight against us for solace and encouragement when times are bad. One such moment for me came that June morning, when over the breakfast table Chris said that one of the good things to have come out of all the anguish and distress he'd felt these last few months, was a clear recognition that he no longer cared who knew about my lifestyle. It was an issue, a fact of life, he no longer felt troubled about.

When he made his speech, he thanked his father and Rita for making the long haul to be present, and then went on to say how much he had appreciated Marie, Meg and his Mother, for having been so supportive, given that he and Catherine had decided to wed in such a hurry (here he paused for the expected laughter), and that he was pleased, very pleased, to have been brought up by these three women who'd looked after him so well.

CATHY BROOKER

I never really wanted to know

I would have been quite happy to continue believing that Louise was just Mum's good friend.

Our first meeting was when I was about nine years old. Mum had gone back to uni now that we were all in school. It was the weekend and our house was untidy, as usual. I recall that the lounge room was full of new bedroom furniture for Mum and Dad's bedroom. An attempt to improve relations in that room, perhaps, that was definitely too late.

Mum introduced us to Louise, an attractive young woman. She wore groovy clothes. I liked her straight away. I was glad for Mum to have a friend, as things hadn't been good between her and Dad for a long time.

From this time, Louise was suddenly everywhere. She came to the movies with us, she was at our house whenever Dad was out (which was a lot of the time), and then she started coming on holidays with us. We went on great holidays, camping, houses down the South Coast. I started to notice that Mum and Louise always shared the same room, the same bed even. Mum's response to my questions was that the only house they could rent had just two bedrooms or that they could only get one tent, which was always pitched about 100 metres away from the van where we slept. My suggestions of Mum sleeping with us and Louise luxuriating in a room of her own were always met with 'valid' excuses.

It used to annoy me the way they'd sit close, whispering and laughing, looking into each others' eyes, having secrets never shared with us. I was jealous. This intruder was much closer to my mother than I ever would be. The big problem was, I had no other reason to dislike her.

Louise seemed to genuinely enjoy spending time with us. She could draw well, and she used to draw us pictures of likeable monsters and friendly dragons and a mutual favourite, cats. She would tell us stories made up from her own imagination. Best of all, she would often forget to curb her language in our presence and we would delight in repeating what we'd heard, *ad nauseam,* in front of Mum.

She liked going to fetes and flea markets, which Mum didn't, and the others were too young, so it was just me and her. I felt special — we'd share the experience of buying kitsch ornaments and bury ourselves in tables of second-hand clothing , and laugh together at Mum's loathing of our new-found treasures. Louise was like a big sister. When Mum wasn't in the car, she'd drive zig-zag down the middle of the road and we'd laugh so hard, especially when one day her crazy fat dog jumped out of the car window and we had to chase her for miles before we caught her.

My brother wasn't so keen on Louise. I don't think it was on account of who she was, but perhaps because she personified the huge rift in our family. He was always sullen in her company and was sometimes rude to her. I don't recall whether he and I ever discussed it, but it was fairly obvious he was not accepting of the situation. My sister had her own ways of demonstrating her feelings. Being the youngest, she was quite close to Mum, and she would actually try to wedge herself between Mum and Louise, and grizzle if she felt jealous.

During my early teenage years I wanted so much to have a 'normal' family, like my friends. Mum and Louise weren't the only aspects of embarrassment surrounding my family. By sixth class, most of the kids in my class knew that my parents didn't get along. My best 'friend' was a particularly nasty girl who alternated between being my friend and my enemy on a fortnightly basis, without reason. On the off-weeks, she'd follow me around with her group of hangers-on and taunt me with, "Your parents are getting a divorce," "Your house is always untidy," and "You haven't *even* got a colour TV!" Maybe if we'd had the telly, the other things might have been more acceptable.

By my early high school years, things had become more strained at home. Mum had moved into a separate room from Dad. She'd also had a lock put on the door, because Dad used to delight in taking stray women in there just to spite her. I think for Dad, the fact that Mum had turned to women was even more difficult to accept. It was as though he thought he'd totally shattered Mum's faith in ever finding a decent man for a partner, and he'd caused her to try women. The door locks didn't stop him, however. It was just more of a challenge for him to get into the room. What must his floozies have made of all this?

At school I regularly dodged questions about my parents' relationship. It was okay now to tell people that my parents had split, but then it was the questions about their new partners. Dad always had some new woman hanging around so he was easy, but Mum! Some weeks I'd say she had a boyfriend, some weeks she didn't have anyone.

But all the while my friends were aware of Mum's constant companion. I still couldn't admit it to myself. I'd find cards with naked women on the outside and mushy messages inside, commencing with 'Dear Chookie', and by now Mum was spending most nights at Louise's house or vice versa.

When I was about fourteen, Louise went to England. I was sad to see her go, but when Mum said she didn't know when Louise was returning, I was secretly happy. Now maybe some normalcy would return to our lives.

I was wrong.

Mum was miserable after Louise's departure. She took up smoking again and drank, sometimes on her own. These were two vices that Louise had persuaded (or was it emotional blackmail?) Mum to give up. Mum had a few other 'friends' whilst Louise was away. She even considered going back to Dad to solve some of the problems. Dad's conditions, however, were that the marriage could resume just as long as he could still see his new girlfriend on weekends.

Louise had been gone about six months when Mum announced she was also going to England. I invited myself along, and was quite excited about the prospect of my first overseas trip.

Mum must've figured it was time. I can still see her, standing by the piano in our lounge room. She didn't really look at me. "If you're coming to England, there's something you should know. Louise and I are lovers." "What the fuck!" I screamed in my mind. "Oh, really," I quietly said. I wanted to be sick. How could she do this to me? It was just my luck. God must hate me! Why couldn't she be like 'normal'

'Louise was like a big sister'

mothers? It was confirmed. I was to be embarrassed for the rest of my life. All these angry thoughts conflicted inside my head, my heart. I think I said, "I had a fair idea," and left.

I don't remember how soon after it was I gave her some feeble excuse as to why I no longer wanted to go to England. I think we both knew the truth. Hell, I was just learning to deal with my own sexuality. I didn't feel strong enough to deal with Mum's as well. Mum was probably secretly relieved, as I now know she had a lot of things to work through with Louise.

I thoroughly enjoyed the time Mum was away. We were farmed out independently to various friends and relatives over the Xmas holidays. I spent that summer chasing boys at discos, dancing, sunbaking for hours at the beach, and even went against my mother's wishes and got my ears pierced. Mum returned from England triumphantly with Louise in tow. Oh great! Here we go again — and I got in trouble for getting my ears pierced!

Mum decided to move out with Louise when I was nearly sixteen. She was taking my younger sister with her, but my brother and I had the choice as to where we wished to live. I chose to stay with Dad, mostly because my school and friends were close by, but also because the problem was going away. My brother also decided to stay. Mum respected our decision. In hindsight it wasn't such a great choice on my part, but the decision to allow us to make our choice as adults was probably a very tough one for Mum.

Dad was pretty irresponsible. He didn't keep a good supply of food in the house, or cook for that matter. My brother and I were responsible for getting ourselves to school on time and running the house. Many nights Dad didn't come home at all. Both our studies suffered.

By sixth form, most of my close friends knew that my mum was gay, and they didn't seem to care. My peers liked me for who I was, and rightly so; Mum's and Louise's relationship didn't affect their opinion of me. My friends liked Mum and Louise, too.

After high school, I could tell anyone I came into contact with and, to my relief, it didn't matter. In fact, at one time Mum's gayness was seen as off-beat and groovy, almost something to be proud of: "Wow, my mum's so boring and 'normal'. What's it like having a gay mum?"

'She's got a gay mum' was almost as good as 'She's got a colour telly'!

I knew, then, that I was old enough to accept my mother's relationship. It had now lasted longer than her marriage to my Dad. She had, and still has, a friend with whom she shares many interests. Louise now has two children for whom my mum is also mum, and they are my little brothers. When we're all together, we're one big noisy family.

Louise's eldest boy is nearly ten, and is starting to receive a fair bit of abuse from the other kids at school about his two mums. I feel sorry for him because, in the nineteen years since I was ten, attitudes haven't changed much. It will be a struggle for him, and there are decisions he has to make about how he's going to handle it. At least I can assure him that in five to six years, hopefully earlier, his friends will accept his mothers' relationship.

We'll see how the next generation goes, now that I am pregnant with Mum's first grandchild. I wonder whether our kids will worry about their two gay nannas? Somehow, I don't think so.

MICHAEL & STEPHANIE BRADSTOCK

Dialogue on the alternative family

S: The homosexual family is probably one of the biggest classes of alternative families, with the least acceptance.

M: I don't think that was much of an issue in our growing up, because I didn't really know about Mum being gay until I was about thirteen. I guess Cathy and I have memories more of drunken uni parties or jazz parties ... I couldn't go to bed yet because there'd be a couple screwing on my plastic sheets. [Laughter]

S: Even that would be alternative to what is accepted. As a young kid our family was very different from other people's families. How did you feel about it at the different stages?

M: I think a lot of families in the '70s were pretty much like that. Should I throw in the bit about being in the same room while Dad's screwing Mum's student who was bisexual? [Laughter]

S: Did you understand that sort of thing at the time?

M: No. No. I thought it was just where Mum sleeps. Which I guess comes to where Louise fitted in a bit later in the piece. I mean, Dad stopped coming away on holidays with us and Louise came along, and when we got five people to a bedroom, two adults and three kids, I didn't think Mum and Louise were sleeping together for any sexual purpose. I guess I thought it was probably just because that's the way they built hotel rooms, and that's the sleeping arrangement we had.

S: So essentially our family didn't become an alternative family until you knew about Mum and Louise's sexuality?

M: I only really discovered that by seeing Mum and Louise in bed together when I was thirteen. I was coming to grips with my own sexuality, and I didn't quite understand; I'd heard about lesbians, I think I'd actually already been told that they were lesbians, but I didn't see anything sexual ...

S: Who would have told you?

M: I think Mum, but I didn't understand relationships at all. A lot of men have a fantasy about watching two women, but when I saw that I guess I rejected Mum for a few years.

S: Did you ever see Mum and Dad sexually active?

M: I guess I saw him grab her tits occasionally. [Laughter]

S: And how did that make you feel?

M: Cause Mum always used to wear [laughter] those black bras. Well, that's the other thing. We were also fairly open about nudity in the family. I mean, nothing unnecessary, more sex education. I remember Mum giving us our sex education lessons. I was probably about seven and I thought it was quite hilarious, but homosexuality wasn't discussed then.

S: So finding out about Mum's sexuality, that's when our family became an alternative family for you, but it's also a point from which you can see a change in your relationship with Mum?

M: I was thirteen, it all happened at once. I found out Mum was a lesbian, Sam [the dog] died, my grandfather died, I lost my virginity. Those last three were all in the one week. I remember Sam dying as being really traumatic, so I guess it was probably more a combination of those things and Dad being such an arsehole. But Cathy and I didn't want to be uprooted, we liked Ryde, we liked the area where we were living. I don't think I saw Louise as the enemy, I guess I did at first but not because of her sexuality, more because she had a militant personality. It felt right to tell her to get fucked because she would tell me to get fucked just as readily. The other thing that makes me sad — everybody likes to feel that in their own way they are their parents' favourite. At least with Mum I knew that she cared about me. I don't think Dad cares one way or the other.

S: He doesn't know what he feels, or he doesn't know how to express it.

M: Mum and I were just starting to get to know each other. Maybe Mum was feeling like she was breaking out from under Dad's thumb at the same time, and then I closed up shop and decided not to get to know her. I think I only started to get back on top of things when I was about nineteen. I know Cathy said the same. But rather than hide it we used to turn it around and 'laugh in the face of adversity', like saying to one of our more hip English teachers on Parent & Teacher night, "Hey, is it alright if your Mum and Dad both bring their girlfriends along?" [Laughter]

S: So you talked about Mum's sexuality to people? Or basically you said it before they could say it? But it was like you were rejecting it as well. I mean, that example sounds like it was a very hip thing to talk about with your English teacher, but what about with the other kids at school?

M: Eventually I came to be seen as a forefront person, you know, blazing a trail through drugs and sex at school. So I could say, "Well, alright, my mum's a dyke, I'm not going to hear any shit about it," rather than people going, "His mum's a lesbian. His sexuality must be suspect too." I don't think I went out on a mad rooting spree or anything …

S: What about losing your virginity at thirteen? Do you think that had anything to do with Mum's sexuality, or was that independent?

M: No, independent. Just curiosity.

S: You underwent quite a change from your primary school, almost persecuted for being the good little boy or for being the studious boy.

M: I wasn't studious, I was just lucky that things came easily to me. I didn't really have to try, and then when I did have to try I didn't have the inclination. Maybe I felt a bit more persecuted then because I had a stigma attached to me — I was supposed to be smart, and therefore I should do well.

S: Like in terms of becoming one of the toughest kids at James Ruse. Can you say how that happened, or why that happened?

M: Probably because I was still hanging round with some of the guys in Ryde East, and I had to do things to be tough in their eyes. I guess I was still a nancy to them by going off to smart school, and getting braces, and I copped a bit at football. I don't know how Jay handles it, he's a lot younger and he's having to deal with it. He seems to be a lot more mature. Well, he's actually been brought up in a gay relationship, but then Mum and Louise are a lot older and they don't have wild parties. We used to go and talk to strange men in the backyard who'd spew round and sleep in the backyard all night. [Laughter]

S: So, as a teenager, was your family noticeably different from other people's families? Did you feel left out or eccentric or weird?

M: The other parents were a lot more involved in what the kids did. I don't know if you found that as well.

S: Yeah, I'd say so. But then perhaps what we gained from it is having parents who were in a way role-models because they both have their own lives, their own interests, whereas other people have parents who don't, and who can want to be too involved.

M: Or maybe they just enjoyed watching their children grow up, and helping them grow up. At the moment it seems like the boys have a lot more input, from what I've seen, than we got.

S: So that's another way our family was different?

M: I guess sometimes Mum tried, but I understand she would have been at the end of her tether, being in that situation with Dad. I don't condone it, but I can understand how some people can be pushed to hit their partner. I'm sure Mum used to really gee Dad up, and I guess

118

you just have to show self-control. It used to make me very angry that Dad hit Mum. I remember hitting him in the belt buckle once and skinning my knuckle, and another time getting great satisfaction from punching him in the lip so he couldn't play his trombone.

S: How did you feel about Mum actually being a lesbian? You said you didn't really talk to her for quite a few years. Do you think that was just adolescence?

M: Maybe. I regard myself as a product of the 'wild and woolly' '70s and coming from a broken marriage, and so it's irrelevant to me, my mother's sexuality now. It couldn't have just been that. Why should I be annoyed at someone for their sexuality? I can't remember the exact reason that I did reject Mum. I can't remember when I started talking to her civilly again. I remember going out with my friend Philip on Friday nights, and I'd have to come over and park myself at Mum's for half an hour and maybe have dinner there. At first I was forced to come home to Mum's place, but once I started to stay out later and later I guess she didn't want me turning in at four or five in the morning. Look at Philip, his parents have just split up in the last three years. As far as I knew they were all happy as Larry, but he was probably just as messed up during his adolescence as I was.

S: You also saw Sally's parents split up perhaps fifteen years after they should have.

M: I don't know that she was screwed up, though. I thought she was fairly level-headed.

S: I just remember the cigarette burns she put into her hands. She had problems.

M: Yeah, but she was on morphine at the time, and there were other kids with problems. I mean, the school was changing. The kids were all doing crazy things, taking drugs. The teachers used to say, "Don't be an idiot, there's lots of kids here come from broken homes, so don't come the poor downtrodden little waif."

S: So you were conscious that you weren't the only one?

M: Yeah, but I don't remember too many. They didn't speak up like I did. Everybody knew, that's Michael, his parents have split up and his mother's a lesbian because he's told us. They might have thought I was nuts or lying ... that was the other thing, it was alright for me to call my mother a dyke, a derogatory term, and put myself down in that way. It's not derogatory now. When you're growing up you do just think of things being male and female. Or I did.

S: I think it was very different for me because I was younger when I found out, and then from first or second year high school, Bella was my best friend and her mother was a dyke. And then I went to a girls' school, and some of the teachers knew Mum and they were gay as well. There was even a suggestion about the headmistress, so I think it wasn't such a different sort of thing. It was also a boarding-school, and some of the girls were a bit *suss* in the way they behaved. I think I was much more aware of the prevalence, inner-city school and that kind of thing. And then amongst my friends at school, out of ten of them eight had broken homes. We had our own little majority out of a minority, we all had a similar situation.

M: As the years wore on there were other people whose parents began to split up, but there were still hard-core 'nice' families.

S: What about your exposure to different sorts of relationship rather than just one sort? Do you think there are any benefits?

M: Well, I'm not prejudiced. Again, it may have taken me a longer period to accept. Say like Rachel's parents who didn't know people had sex before marriage until their son had two illegitimate children to two different women. And they didn't even know about homosexual relationships or didn't acknowledge they existed until Rachel was living with a lesbian couple, and her brother despises fags. A lot of people say, "Oh god, look at those fags." They don't bother me at all, they're just happy. A lot of people blame homosexuals for the AIDS virus. Who do we blame, the randy men from Haiti who had sex with monkeys?

S: No comment.

M: I can't say I've got any close homosexual male friends. The girl who lives at Rachel's place, I'm quite friendly with her. And the girl from Canada, when we went to visit her I got on like a house on fire with her girlfriend. She thought it was funny we had an ice cream called a Gaytime.

S: Even though you weren't living with Mum in your teenage years, we all still went on our family holidays together.

M: Yes, I remember the last holiday we all went on together ... I guess I just looked at that as a gift-horse. I don't think I was aggressive towards Mum, just apathetic. A lot of teenagers are. But the root of it was because my mother wasn't like other mothers.

S: Do you feel there's some sort of duplicity present in a more conventional lifestyle, that perhaps wasn't present in ours?

M: Just look at —'s [a well-known Christian fundamentalist's] kids. His daughter was the town bike at some sort of Youth & Rec. camp that Sally went on, and his son's branded as a 'hopeless druggie', with all the strong moral upbringing he gave them. If he'd loosened up a bit, his kids could have come to him with their problems. I'd like to think, now that all the hoo-hah's died down, I could still go and talk to Mum about problems. I guess there was an interesting conversation I had about a year ago with Mum, about the thrill of the chase, the sexual conquest or whatever, and when she first saw Louise. I'm glad that Mum can be open with me like that now, but maybe she couldn't expect us to comprehend anything she would have wanted to say back then. Now they're saying as much as possible to Jay. It's a lot for a nine year old boy to deal with, but in the long run he'll understand a lot more. Who knows, he may end up being homosexual himself, or he might end up rebelling. I don't think I actually rebelled and became a tough guy, because I wasn't really tough ...

S: I think probably what the three of us had was just knowledge. We knew about sex and about drugs ... just from talking about things, being exposed to things. So it was more that credibility from having knowledge.

M: That was the other thing that we had. Us three were fairly close through our teenage years, although you started to drift away when you used to stay more with Mum and Louise.

S: We still had the weekends of parties, and going up the pub.

M: Was that after you left school?

S: No, I was about thirteen. I was never a drinker, though.

M: So ... through our lack of parental guidance we tended to guide ourselves, and I don't think we've turned out all that badly.

TERESA SAVAGE

Sharp hair and mother-blaming

"Y ou got dogs or babies?"

What Angie needed was a haircut, not an interrogation. But I'd recently heard a news item on the ABC about TAFE incorporating counselling skills into its hairdressing courses — and I wasn't going to be left behind. Maybe she would have preferred silence, but she wasn't going to get it.

"All the lesbians in Leichhardt have dogs or babies." Angie tried to turn her head but I had her skull in a vice. "I'm telling you it's true. And I see a lot of them." I trundled the razor up the back of Angie's neck. Right first go. She'd got both.

It was a new condition for her. She'd been where wedlock turns to padlock. Out in the suburbs for years, eventually realising that the smile of the woman in the dry-cleaner's was more important to her than the grunt of thanks she got when she hung his clean suit in the built-in. She knew she had to leave PaulPeteBob. Sell the house, divide up the money. And where was she to go? Leichhardt of course, her straight friends said, if that's what you're going to be.

motherless: *without a mother.*

You know, even in Leichhardt you can feel isolated. Stroll up Norton Street with a bag of groceries, a child on either side and the dog cocking its leg at every garbage can and you wonder if you're an impostor. Angie settled the children into the local school. She joined the library and idly typed the word *lesbian* into the catalogue. She thought of learning Italian. She visited the local doctor and said 'none needed' when asked about contraception. After all this she knew she had to find others like herself. The Women's Health Centre gave her a phone number. She dredged up what courage she had left and rang. The woman on the other end sounded friendly enough. Said she'd meet her next day at Bar

Italia, when the kids were at school.

Bar Italia, with its flapping noticeboard — *Dyke wanted for cosy creative household in Petersham.* With its eccentric mix of literati, lesbians and liberals it holds on to its reputation for serving the best coffee and the smoothest gelato in Sydney. Amnesty International holds its monthly meetings there. Publishers, journalists and film producers arrange tete-a-tetes. Mothers feed ice-cream to small kids in strollers. And occasionally you see lovers, crouched over in corners, pushed against the grimy public telephone or the glass fronted room where fruit is pureed in great metal vats.

Angie didn't know how she'd recognise the woman. Perhaps she should have used the old red carnation trick. But it didn't matter — there was only one woman alone there, a woman with a mass of natural curls. She sat at a table in the corner, huddled over a book and a half-finished cappuccino. "You Angie?" She rose from her seat, "I'm Tess." Nodding toward the counter, she asked, "What do you want?" The lean guy who pulled the coffee obviously knew her. Angie couldn't catch what he said but he sloped towards Tess as he spoke, and laughed out loud at her reply. Angie pulled over the book on the table. It was called *We are everywhere.* Tess handed her a flat white. "Now, what can I do for you?"

mothercraft: *the knowledge and skill associated with the rearing of children.*

Turns out Tess had been a lesbian mother for years. Children can be a kind of inevitable by-product of marriage — you know, have the wedding, have the house, have the baby — the natural consequence of a heterosexual partnership. But not for Tess and her partner Libby. They had to search out the wherewithal, work out the mechanics, fight their way through the obstetrics machine, invent defences to meet the inevitable criticisms. And now Tess had become an ambassador of a kind, giving talks and writing papers, shaking her wild tresses all around town — what's known to us as networking. But still angry. At the time she met Angie her theory of lesbian mothering was still evolving. Well, one aspect in particular.

"Mother-blaming," she said. Angie didn't quite catch that. She raised her eyebrows, knowing Tess was some way down the track from her. "It's like we've fallen into a trap set up for us by the destructive ideology of the nuclear family," Tess said, sounding as though she was leading a workshop. "Criticising mothers is fair game. All those mother-in-law jokes are the extreme end of it, and I object to them." Angie wondered about herself, if she objected, or if she would next time her fuckwit brother-in-law made a stupid crack. Tess rushed on — I'm surprised she didn't pull out her lecture notes. "I just see it all the time. There's such a deep level of mother hatred rampant out there. Mothers are blamed for every failing of the adult child. Relationships, career, artistic appreciation … do you know what I mean?" When she said it like that Angie had to agree. It had already occurred to her that in ten years' time she might need to re-mortgage the house to pay for the kids' therapy. But Tess was on a roll, "And do we lesbians do it too? Yes we do. While we champion the oppression of women everywhere else, we refuse to see the extenuating circumstances of our own mothers' lives, how they too had to survive. I don't know about yours, but mine was certainly suffering in a rotten marriage. She had very little room for growth or independence." Angie could tell it was going to be a long session.

"I mean," Tess was pushing her curls up at the back, giving herself a scalp massage, "I mean, so many women I know, loads of them real radical lesbian feminists, carry on seeing the source of their adult difficulties as their own mother." Angie squirmed with what must have been guilt. "At the same time, they all love their fathers, or at least admire them." Did Angie love hers? More a case of mutual indifference. "I mean. You're at a party or something. A woman only has to mention that her mother's coming to stay and other women raise their eyebrows knowingly. Nod their heads. Oooo, that must be terrible. Have you noticed that?" Angie blinked. "I'll get us more coffee."

While she was gone Angie dragged her spoon around the empty cup and tried to work it out. It was like the two notions of lesbian and mother were somehow opposite. Even she'd been around long enough to realise that the Amazon image, the big-tough-bike-riding-boot-kicking-gal didn't sit too well with the domestic-sacrificing-slave-making-a-caramel-slice-for-their-aftenoon-tea. And maybe that was the point. Divide and rule.

But Tess was back, balancing two overflowing cups in her jaunty style. "What time do you have to go? I pick mine up at three-twenty." She checked her Swatch. "We've got a bit of time yet." Angie was enjoying herself. She felt exhilarated, even decadent, sitting in a cafe in the middle of the day discussing ideas, theories, abstract things. Even if she was doing a lot of listening. Because Angie, being a well-brought-up girl, is a good listener. Tess was obviously flattered — but only for a moment. No doubt that was the kind of thing she basked in later. "And another thing," she carried on, "we lesbians, like the rest of the world, seem to hold very strong views about good and bad mothering. And anyone — 'specially men, who've got no idea of the day-to-day juggling act that most mothers perform," Tess mimed a juggler's swinging arms, "anyone feels free to express their criticism of mothers. It astonishes me."

Angie knew what she meant. Even the dog's bad behaviour was her fault. "I mean, I was on a bus once, in London this was. I had my son, he was only a baby. I had him in one of those carry slings, you know." Angie must have nodded. "I mean who could negotiate public transport in London with a pram? But I struggle onto the bus, plonk down in my seat and this woman opposite says to me, you'll damage that child's spine for life, carrying it around like that. Damage it for life. And instead of pointing out to her that in that case all the children in Africa, India and goddess knows where else should be crippled, I sit there in silence, worrying that I've done the wrong thing. You know. Total angst. New mother angst," and she stared into her coffee, "damaged him for life. That happened to you?"

We've all seen the woman in the supermarket who recommends a good slap as a remedy for a child demanding lollies from the child's-eye-level display stand — or the father at the swimming pool whose children run to him in fear when he calls, who whispers slyly when yours dawdle, you see, they respond to a man's authority.

mother-fucker: *a person or thing which arouses exasperation, irritation, contempt etc.*

"And what makes me laugh is that quite often my childless friends do it too. They just can't see the connection. I've been thinking lately that I'll start criticising their performance at work. Tell them they're ruining the public service for life. What do you reckon?"

It was time to go. Pick up the kids and take them to gym, their piano lesson, basketball …

mother: *a term of familiar address for an old or elderly woman.*

Angie thought about Tess a lot that week. It was her habit to look in the dark corners. Angie's own mother, in a floral full-bodied apron, was always standing in the kitchen, a wire tray of fresh pikelets on the bench beside her. It took Angie a great deal of energy to blow that away. But now here she was, happy to be re-modelled by new ideas. But she still kept hold of some of the old ones.

If a thing's worth doing, do it well. That's what her mum had said. Angie'd taken that one to heart. That's what comes of being a Capricorn I suppose.

mothercraft: *the knowledge and skill associated with the rearing of children.*

That was the week Angie decided that her six year old was too big to come into her bed every night. Too big and too awkward, throwing her arms and legs around, one elbow up under her mother's ribs and lying diagonal across the bed. What gorgeously eligible woman would want to share a bed with her and a nocturnal octopus? So, this was it, she had to take a stand with Amy. She dragged the child back to her own bed, perched on the edge and listened to her whimpering. She knew she was re-writing the plot. Amy would probably have a pattern of choosing people who rejected her. Even people who abused her. For Angie it was a revelation to realise she had so much power.

Something else happened to Angie that week. It was that peculiar phenomenon of like attracting like. You know, the human magnet — the pregnant woman who spends her day crossing paths with other pregnant women; the unfaithful wife who catches the eye of another woman across the desk and knows that she too is treading the path of desire and deceit and ultimate destruction. That week Angie saw the whole world intent on a mission to blame all mothers for every fraying seam in the social fabric.

mother superior: *the head of a female religious community.*

Next time they'd arranged to meet, Angie arrived first. She sat at a table and read the notices, trying to look inconspicuous. Tess was late. But then Angie saw her, the curly head poking through the doorway. "Shall we walk this time? I brought the dog."

It was a Maltese terrier. Bandy-legged, white and fluffy. What Angie's father would call a poof dog.

Down past the Civic Video, with its gaudy yellow and blue stripes, past a few houses in Federation green and cream, and up the sandstone steps into Pioneers Park. That took care of the pleasantries.

"But why does it happen?" Angie asked. "What function does it have?"

"Blaming mothers oppresses women," Tess replied in a bored, tired kind of way — she must've said it a thousand times. "But what it also does is divert us from looking at all the things which cause childhood trauma." She bent and unclipped Snowy from his leash. "I mean, when you think about it, who in reality damages children?" The question was rhetorical. Angie waited. Tess was winding the leash around and around her hand. "Men. Incest. Violence." She dropped her arm and the leash slowly unwound. "And they do it in an indirect way as well. They have a great knack for not engaging, keeping their emotional distance, encouraging competition between mother and daughter."

Have you noticed how mothers who remain silent are somehow more to blame for violating the child than the abusive father? Neglect of maternal duty is the real crime.

Tess picked up a stick and threw it for Snowy. He ignored it, so she bounded off and retrieved it herself. "Here Snow," she said as she pushed the stick into his mouth. He immediately dropped it and raced off to sniff a cocker spaniel's tail. "Hopeless." She was winding the leash again.

Angie could tell that Tess's mind was moving on, straining to make connections. "I'm beginning to think that this is particularly important for lesbians. Particularly lesbian mothers. Particularly lesbian mothers of daughters."

Ideas with no obvious connection can be pushed, jettisonned into their own orbit to intersect with others, creating their own arcs, their own overlapping sectors. The ridges on the trunk of a tree, a strand of hair falling on a bare shoulder, the circle of her watch-face.

"Sorry. I'm always like this," she grinned. "Woman raves on in park. I earbash all my friends. Get an idea and I can't let it go. Unlike the dog." Snowy was cocking his leg up a wrinkly old gum tree.

"But why would we want to contribute to an ideology which separates mothers and daughters?" Angie asked. "That's what's been bugging me all week."

Tess was quiet for a moment, tugging at one ear. "What everyone seems to have missed is that the mother daughter relationship is a woman to woman relationship, full of all kinds of revolutionary potential."

This idea hit Angie hard. They'd reached the rotunda, and she slumped down on the cement steps. A 440 bus pulled out of the garage and chugged down the road. Tess continued. "Surely we should all be doing what we can to maintain close relationships between mothers and daughters. It would move us all forward. Young women could adapt our insights, instead of finding it all out again the hard way." Tess wandered off to find Snowy.

Poor old Angie's head was churning. But she could see the point. Her own mother had told her once that the measure of a good mother is a good daughter. She knew that meant she had to be compliant — make the most of her looks — be absolutely heterosexual. She suddenly felt sorry for her mother — no hope now. And then Angie's own daughter, bound up with her six year old concerns. She knew that if she would never be judged a good mother, then Amy would never be judged a good daughter.

Tess reappeared, with Snowy on the leash. "I've got to go now. Loads to do."

They wandered over to Norton Street. Angie asked if they could meet again the next week. "Love to," Tess laughed. "I'm really enjoying working all this out. Maybe we should write an article or something?" And she took off down the street, Snowy scrabbling at her heels and occasionally nipping at her Blundstones.

mother: *to acknowledge oneself the author of or assume as one's own.*

It's strange how one person can affect another. Not in a threatening way, but in a way which throws new light, changes the angles, so that every past decision, every aspect of style, is somehow altered in retrospect.

That week Angie even tried to teach her dog to fetch a stick. But what she mostly thought about, at night after she'd put the children to bed, was the lack of community control and interest in the lives of children. Her son wet the bed two nights running.

motherland: *one's native country or the land of one's ancestors.*

She longed to be part of a larger group, to live in a supportive community. It was this that she had lost. In the fifties, that golden cage of domestic nostalgia, mothers would turn to their own mothers, their neighbours, the local shop-keeper, for advice and practical help. Now Angie's neighbours were at work or at the movies. Her own mother lived far away, and in any case their views were now so disparate that Angie despised the constant maternal platitudes based on keeping women and children in a helpless and hopeless place. Angie knew that a woman is known by the company she keeps.

The phone rang while she was pegging out the sheets. She raced in from the yard, tripping up the back step and crashing one elbow against the door frame.

"I thought you weren't home."

"Hanging out the laundry," she mumbled apologetically. "How are you Tess?"

"Good. Wondering if you'd like to come over to dinner Saturday night. Bring the kids. Libby'd like to meet you."

"Saturday?" she hesitated. Didn't want to jump immediately. Eagerness in accepting invitations can imply weakness, a habitual state of vulnerable void. "Saturday. Yes. That'd be good."

"Come about six. That way we can feed the kids and still have time to talk. And, oh yes, we're vegetarian. That okay with you?" Predictable in a way, but also brave, and difficult. My transcendental meditator cousin once said she thought being vegetarian was the cutting edge of difference, the first pointer to social eccentricity, particularly in the land of the barbecued snag and the steak sandwich. "I'll see you Saturday then."

mother's boy: *a boy or man who is excessively attached to his mother and often somewhat effeminate.*

She arrived exactly on time. Amy marched up the path happily, but David stayed close. She'd told him they were going to spend the evening

128

with some lesbians and their children. He wasn't sure if he wanted to be part of it. Confronting children with the stark reality of their situation isn't always best. Angie was hoping he'd like the other children. Being a bit of a softy, David tagged along without complaining.

Tess opened the door. She was obviously in mid-sentence, but paused while she let them pass her into the hallway. "We were just laughing about what happened today at the shoe shop."

"This is David," Angie pushed him forward, "and that one's Amy." Amy was already lying on the floor scratching Snowy behind the ears.

"And this is Libby." Tess linked her arm through the elbow of a small woman with stunning hair — blonde, very straight and cropped into what used to be called a shingle. Libby had a tea-towel slung over one shoulder. She poured Angie a glass of wine.

"We had to take these three to buy new shoes." She waved one arm in the direction of a tall boy draped over an arm chair, his legs dangling over the side and a book over his face. "Always a horrific experience, particularly if you are hung up like we are on good shoes with good support and growing room." Her enunciation was wonderfully exaggerated. "We spent the best part of an hour with this shop assistant. She was very friendly, very patient, very helpful. But I could see that flicker in the back of her eye, couldn't you Lib?" Libby nodded, her yellow hair flopping back and forth — no styling mousse there. Tess went on, "Well, she waited until she could buttonhole me. I was at the counter, paying the bill, you know letting the friction heat up the old bankcard, when she suddenly asked me which child belonged to me." A sturdy girl about ten years old appeared and leant against the door jamb. Tess glanced at her, then turned again to me. "What was interesting was that in the moment before I answered, all I was aware of was three sets of eyes glued to me. Three sets of ears wagging. Bit like now, eh Megan?" The girl in the doorway grinned and slid down to crouch on the polished floorboards. "So I decided to use what I call my charming approach." Tess raised her shoulders and pushed out her breasts. "Oh yes, I said, our family is very unusual. We all live together. We share the children."

"And what did the assistant say?" Angie asked.

"She said, 'that's good'. And gave me a beaming false smile." Tess took a gulp of her wine. "The point was that I wasn't answering for her benefit, I don't owe her anything. And I wasn't answering for mine or Lib's." Even the boy was listening now, his book dangling open in one hand. "I was answering for theirs."

mother's ruin: *gin or aunty's downfall.*

Angie enjoyed that evening. Something about being with them made her feel animated, like all her receptive wires were stripped back to bare metal. Angie wanted to be told everything.

They told her about pain. Pain the children feel when they know about hurt inflicted on their mothers. About how in that knowing they learn to empathise with other people, to understand the structure of the system which keeps anyone different powerless. How the kids learn to acknowledge and express their own fears and loves, and to recognise ours. And how sometimes they feel the need to ease the pain for us.

Tim, the big boy joined in: "Yeh, other kids tease me, and sometimes they hit me, but it's nothing much. I think I'm really lucky to have two mums." Course he is, but he shouldn't have to put up with it.

And Megan said, "It's okay really, but it can be really slack. I just wish they'd stop asking me who my real mum is."

About eleven o'clock, after they'd eaten, the kids curled up around the TV in the sitting room. The three women hadn't moved from the table, sitting there surrounded by dirty plates, cold spaghetti hardening into question marks.

Libby was expounding on the subject of daughters. "To work out what we want to do differently, we have to look at what girls learn from traditional mothering," she said, rising from the table. Tess began to stack the plates. "What was it I read the other day? That to be a successful daughter you need to learn to cater to male supremacy — to serve and submit — to give way to the authority of the father and the brother. It's exhausting, all that energy going out. In the end what they do is love everyone except themselves." She paused, halfway to the sink, a pile of plates in her hands, the cutlery finely balanced. Libby had obviously been reading the work of Alice Miller. She knew about the ways in which patriarchal family patterns can stifle children's vitality and repress suffering. She knew that this repression destroys our ability to feel empathy for the suffering of others. And she knew she did not want that for her own children.

"What we have to do is recognise the inevitable pattern, that daughters learn their mothering skills by absorbing their own mothers' mothering." She stopped at the sink. "I mean, how often have you found yourself saying something to the children, and you stop yourself. Look over your shoulder. That wasn't me who just said that, it was my mother." She turned and reached for the plug. "This is what's really exciting. What in the seventies, if we'd thought of it, we would have called the revolutionary potential of lesbian mothering. We just don't do it. We refuse to maintain the status quo. We break traditional patterns, and replace them with other, more woman-centred ones. Then we are transmitting our patterns or values for generations to come." She was facing the sink now, her hands sloshing about in the soapy water. "Anyway, do you want some coffee?"

mother tongue: *the language first learned by a person, their native language.*

With David and Amy slumped on the back seat Angie drove through the quiet streets of Leichhardt, headlights picking out rotting weatherboards and cement-rendered verandahs. She was high on Libby's ideas. Looking up at the stars which are sometimes vibrant despite Sydney pollution, she could imagine all the mother-daughter ties, stretching through space and cloud and air and smog and blood into the future. The impression of a star, its light, leaves the burning object in an act of faith, venturing through the darkness to penetrate a human eye. Do you understand the concept of light years? It's a concept that has no everyday meaning, not in Leichhardt anyway. What Angie was struggling with was a sense of herself as an active star, able to transmit her impression into unknown future territory.

motherlove: *unconditional enduring love.*

Angie realised that by acting as role models, lesbians could teach girls the possibilities of loving women. They could experience the safety of women's company. They could learn to love themselves against the outside judgements of race, size, age, ability, and looks. Lesbian mothers, by living independently, could teach children that women can be resourceful. "We show them a wide range of possibilities," she said to herself. David stirred and mumbled something in his sleep. "They see us knitting and sewing and building and fixing cars." She was kidding herself here — she can't even open the bonnet of her Corolla. "I suppose what's most important is that girls could learn from lesbians to avoid competing for male attention. God knows I spent enough time doing that." She cruised up to park outside her house, still surprised at where she was living.

When Angie flicked off the engine there was silence. During the day Leichhardt roars with the planes on their flightpath to the airport, so that at night it seems unnaturally quiet, while the curfew lasts that is. Carrying the sleeping Amy to her bed was not too bad, but David was bigger. His head slumped back over her arm as she negotiated the hallway, careful not to knock him against the door of his room. As she rolled him under his racing car doona he opened his eyes. "Goodnight Mum," he whispered. "Goodnight Sunshine," she whispered back. Angie is living proof that there is only one pretty child in the world, and every mother has it — in this case two.

She couldn't sleep. Maybe she needed company, but back then there was none on offer. Maybe she needed someone to love her body — but not in a gentle way. What she needed was fierce and passionate — I've learnt that now. But back then she couldn't stop thinking about her choices in life and where they had brought her. In the kitchen, perched on a stool, she stared out into the dark yard. She didn't need a drink. She was full.

That long night Angie decided several things:

She decided to always challenge instances of mother-blaming.

She decided to empower her daughter by encouraging warmth, passion, strength and the ability to work with others.

She decided that she would never again consider her children to be her property. (She must have laughed aloud at the use of the possessive pronoun.)

She decided to acknowledge that children are one of the most powerless groups in our society.

What had brought her to this point? She was suddenly aware of the lack of choice children have over basic aspects of their lives, how their sexuality is denied, how they endure total financial dependence, how meagre their legal rights seem, and how they are at the mercy of the whims and vagaries of the personalities of their parents, teachers and all adults. Not unlike her own former state with PaulPeteBob.

She realised that the children of lesbians never see themselves, or their lifestyles, reflected in books, on TV, in educational resources. They live in a world which estranges them by making them strange. She knew about feeling cornered, frustrated, negated by the world. And what could she do with that feeling? She resolved to be wary of transmitting that frustration within her relationships — particularly in relation to those less powerful than her.

The sky was lightening over the tin roof of the next-door neighbour's shed. At last she relaxed. More than relaxed, she felt spent. She staggered fully clothed into her room and fell into bed.

Three hours later Angie was aware of Amy curled beside her. "Read me a book, Mum." Angie moaned, and turned her back. "Come on Mum. I've got this new library book from school." Angie could feel the sharp corner of the book in the fleshy part of her ear.

"Just let me sleep a bit longer," she pleaded. Amy dropped out of bed and stomped around to her side. She pulled up one of Angie's eyelids with her insistent fingers.

"Mum, come on. You said you would read to me on Sunday mornings. You musn't break a promise." She let the eyelid droop, but her voice was angry. "Come on Mum." And then Angie wondered what to do when the lessons have been so well learnt? When her assertive daughter confronts her continually, just as she's been taught to do? Angie heaved herself up and took the book from her daughter.

"Come on then." She patted the pillow. "What's this book about?"

Later she got up and wrote it all down. Kept it in a notebook on her bedside table. Not that I read other people's notebooks, you understand. But I know she wrote it down.

The following week she had another haircut. Sharp hair was part of the new Angie — out on the street, engaging with it all.

"So, how's it going in sunny Leichhardt?" I asked, tying a black cape around Angie's neck.

"Great." She must have been feeling brave. "Good. Do you like kids?"

JANET PETERS

When I woke up I was in Thailand

I. *Chiang Mai*

August 1993 — off on our three week trip to Fiji. I hope our one year old daughter will travel well. I hope I can manage looking after her by myself for two weeks while my lover, her mother, is working. I feel queasy in the evenings.

December 1993 — four months pregnant and having Christmas at my lover's parents' place in Canberra. We want a change in our lives. She wants to change jobs after nine years with the same outfit. I just feel restless. We think about jobs in Darwin. Her father hands her a scrap of newspaper, saying, "This sort of thing might be interesting for you."

January 1994 — she says, "This job is in Chiang Mai, should I apply for it?" I think, why not, it's good interview practice, and Chiang Mai isn't that much further than Darwin, is it?

May 1994 — our second daughter is born, plump, healthy and beautiful.

July 1, 1994 — the four of us, our daughters aged 22 months and eight weeks, my lover and me, board British Airways Flight 1 to Bangkok for the connecting flight to Chiang Mai, and a two year contract. I hope I can manage looking after two children by myself for two years while she works.

So we all know by now that the institution of the family relies on the oppression of women to supply domestic services. We all know that being a dependent spouse can lead to neurosis, depression, loss of self-confidence and self-esteem. But this is different, isn't it?

We're in a mutually supportive relationship. I have a good job in Sydney which will give me leave for two years to go with her to Thailand. We resolved together that we wanted a change from Sydney life, and I wasn't going to be working anyway with a small baby. Terrific, we could enrol the by-then two year old in a posh Thai kindy (good for acquiring a second language). I can stay home with the baby and with a *phi liang* to help with child care, I could work on my tennis game and get fit, catch up on a bit of reading, lovely!

We sell the car, store our furniture and rent out the house. Frenzy of packing, sorting stuff for storage or shipping. The removalists arrive while I'm trying to feed the baby and take the toddler to child care. The baby sleeps surrounded by cardboard boxes and the removalists pack the saucepan on the stove still full of food. Don't these guys think?

Rush of form-filling to get the baby's birth certificate in time to get her passport in time to get the tickets in time to depart. The day of departure arrives — where are the tickets? Have you got the passports? Which queue is moving fastest? The toddler is travelling well until she has to get out of the pram to walk through airport security. She starts screaming with stress and tiredness. I can understand that, I could go for a good wail myself. At last, we're on the plane, we made it, everything's going to be OK.

Bangkok passes in a blur, and Chiang Mai looks beautiful from the air. We stay in a hotel while looking for a house. Nothing in our price range. Next price bracket, and we find one that's OK, except it has no telephone. Don't worry, says the landlord, it will be connected soon. We buy a car, sight unseen, from a departing embassy family in Bangkok. It's fine, very comfy and has air con and central locking.

We employ a *phi liang* and look around for a kindergarten. Still no phone. The embassy sends up some information about the settling-in process for relocating families. First a period of wild excitement, everything's new and interesting. Then fear and anxiety — is this environment safe and healthy? Are the medical services OK? Then life becomes normal, the new normal.

We live in Chiang Mai.

II. *Occupation — Housewife*

Reality check — the new normal arrives. I'm a dependent spouse, in a country where I can't speak the language, and there are no visible single mothers, let alone lesbian mothers. We're in the closet for the first time in our relationship. Always the questions: "And where do you work?" "Uh well, I'm just at home with the kids." "I'm helping my friend who's a single mother like me." "Where's your husband?" "Uh well, he died." "He left." "I'm not married." I forget which story I've told to whom.

Depression sets in. I find myself socialising with embassy wives and white South African women whose husbands work for tobacco companies. My tennis opponent is the wife of the Australian Federal Police officer based in Chiang Mai on drug surveillance. (Ye Gods!) The local gym is full of men strutting and preening in front of the mirrors.

I'm not sure I can handle this. I think I have to go home. Still no telephone. The only thing that saves me is the near constant stream of visitors from home. Luckily, we at least had the sense to go to a city which is on the main tourist routes.

I feel like I'm living my life vicariously through my lover. She's my interpreter for conversations. She translates TV shows as there isn't any English language TV or radio. Still no phone, so our friends and family call her at work and she tells me about it when she comes home. I have no job, so no identity and nothing to talk about except the kids or her job. She's working in AIDS prevention and care. Yes, it must be very interesting for her. The mail is bad and we lose letters, so we tell everyone to write to her office. So then I have to ask each day, did we get any letters?

Gradually, we get used to the climate. We leave town during the hot season. The second rainy season is better than the first, although it rains more and the whole of the north and northeast is flooded. We decide to be 'out' to *farangs,* non-Thais, but stay in the closet to Thais. The mothers' group copes very well with a dyke in their midst; I know they know because I came out to a couple of people and at the next playgroup, everyone is *terribly nice* to me. I host the next playgroup and *everyone* comes.

My lover goes to a meeting and the Thai co-ordinator is wearing a lesbian pride badge. Suddenly we're out to our first Thai, and it's hard to know who's more excited, she or us. We hear through the gay gossip that 'a prominent business woman' is a dyke. Our new dyke friend arranges an introduction and the prominent business woman comes to dinner and we like her a lot.

At the end of the first year, we decide to go home to Sydney for a holiday. I think maybe I won't come back for our second year. But the time comes and we do go back. But now I think it has to be different. I can't go on like this.

So I apply for jobs at the International Schools and get asked at interview if I'm married, do I have children, how old is your daughter, who will look after your baby while you work? The Principals remark that she's very young to be left with a carer for so long. No job offers. I never thought I'd be asked questions like that at a job interview.

Is it because of my lack of a husband? Or don't I have enough teaching experience? Then a *farang* friend says she is leaving to go home to the States. Do I want to take over her job at the University? When I get asked again where is my husband, I say he's in Australia and I miss him a lot. I get the job.

July 1, 1995 — I start work. I'm not a housewife any more.

III. *The Last Year*

August 1994 — she says, "I know I'm not going to want to go home when my contract is finished. It's too short a time to be here." We talk about extending her contract. How will it affect the kids? Is the environment healthy? Should I resign from my job at home in Sydney?

We workshop extending her contract and staying on. We decide to stay if I can get more leave. I write and ask for another eight months leave. Personnel writes back that the leave is approved. Where would we be without the public service?

My job at the University is going well. I'm the only 'foreigner' (non-Thai) in a workplace of 230 people. I took lessons in *wai-ing*, so I could show respect to the Dean at work. Luckily I work in an all-female environment. On the advice of my lover, I buy sweets for the secretaries. It works and everyone relaxes with the 'foreigner'. They tell me I'm *riap roi* (orderly, quiet and well-mannered). Little do they know! Everyone is friendly and positive.

Then the rainy season is on in earnest. The roads flood and fall apart. The municipality decides not to collect the rubbish as they have nowhere to dispose of it. The streets fill with rubbish, it floats down the gutters with the flooding rains in huge smelly clumps. Rats appear. We worry about disease. The city stinks.

The three year old strikes trouble at school. She can't write her letters. She cries every day and won't go to school. Should we send her to the International School? We interview principals and teachers, anxiously and incessantly talk about it at home. How can we decide? There's no one to talk it over with. Eventually we mention it to the teacher. She goes into overdrive to reassure the three year old and us. It all goes back to normal. Sighs of relief.

The baby, now a toddler, is falling over a lot. I mention it to a friend who's a doctor. He suggests a brain scan to rule out a brain tumour. The local specialist thinks it could be epilepsy. Doctors here like to diagnose the Big Condition. We hover over the baby as she sleeps, worrying and crying. If only someone was here to give us some support. The scan reveals a minor abnormality. Nothing to worry about, she says reassuringly.

The toddler, now 18 months old, starts school. Real school, with uniforms, singing the national anthem and learning letters. She goes off with her sister each day in her uniform, looking unbearably cute, wearing a nappy and clutching a bottle. She takes her *phi liang* to school with her, too — the baby princess. The school appears to accept the two mothers phenomenon. As the only 'foreigners' at the school, maybe we're off the weirdness scale, and anyway families are much more fluid here. The three year old is deputised by the teachers to look after her baby sister, no questions asked. The kids learn Thai dancing and say prayers to the Buddha each morning.

With the cooler, dry weather, the party season starts in earnest. The firecrackers are loud and constant. Young men sit outside to play guitars, sing love songs and play flutes. The students play loud music till three a.m.

Next door holds a merit making ceremony, raising money for the temple. Money in an envelope is put in the silver offering tray. The school traditional instrument band shows up and plays. Food, firecrackers, beer and balloons. Curious, we show up for an hour, eat some burningly hot spice noodles and then take the kids home to bed. They raise a huge amount of money and we all have a lot of fun.

We have to decide about staying on for another three years. Should I resign? I don't think any more leave is possible. Do you really want to stay another three years? I don't know, do you? Ambivalence on all sides.

Our dyke friend tells us a new Thai lesbian group is forming in Chiang Mai. Do we want to come to the meeting? Of course we do! After the meeting we go out to dinner. The Thai dykes love the kids. We arrange to go to the *Loy Kratong* festival together next month.

But we miss our friends. *Lesbians on the Loose* arrives and reminds us that Sydney has a big dyke community. Big brouhaha about the Lesbian Space Project. From this distance I can't understand the fuss. The *Sydney Morning Herald* arrives from the Embassy. Big article on lesbian families. 8.7% of dykes have kids, and 20% think they'll have them in the next five years. Hmm.

We're comfortable here now. We've met and conquered adversity together. We have a good income, astronomical by local standards. Our house in Sydney is under the third runway. The weather is nicer here. The kids are happy.

Expatriate friends we've made here are starting to leave. It's a transient life. Embassy staff change posts, University people go home to good career prospects and fat salary packages, others have just had enough of Thailand and pack up.

We decide against staying. This is our last year.

SASHA SOLDATOW

Where have all the sperm gone?

Interviewed by Louise Wakeling at Gary Dunne's 40th birthday party in Bondi.

L: Sasha, you haven't given generously during these years of the lesbian baby boom — why not?

S: That is a really complex question to start off with. I thought you might end with that one! [Laughter]

L: I gather you're concerned gay men might want to be increasingly involved in the nurturing of their donored children?

S: That's not a concern about all gay men, that's one of *my* concerns. It's interesting, actually, with Gary. He talks about 'my baby', when really all that he's done is put some sperm in a bottle. I like kids a lot, I think they're terrific, but I know perfectly well I would be a horribly doting father.

L: Do you think this is a danger, that some gay men might become too emotionally involved?

S: I think there are two problems. One problem is when the kids grow up. For example, if you mix up three or four men's sperm, kids want to know what their background is. That's a real problem — adopted kids also want to know, and now they've got the right to. The other problem is that there has to be almost a legal pact. If the mother does not want the involvement of the father, it should be spelt out right from the very beginning. Emotionally, I think I would find that a problem, not beforehand, but after the child was born.

L: From what I know about various lesbian couples and their unofficial contractual arrangements with gay men, these sorts of things are spelt out well before the donoring actually happens. In the past, gay men didn't have a problem with saying, "I don't need to have any more than an uncle role, if that's necessary," or "I don't need to be involved at all, I'm just doing you this favour out of a political motivation." But there seems to have been a change of heart in the last few years, where gay men are beginning to re-think that position quite seriously.

S: Taking on nurturing roles.

L: Yes, realising, "Hey, in twenty years' time, I'm going to be wondering, do I have any children out there? Maybe I want to know them, and maybe I've missed out on something," the way many straight fathers have missed out on fathering.

S: I'll be 67, though. [Laughter] I'll feel as though I've missed out on a lot, much more than that! A lot of that sort of problem is, for me, fantasy. I have this fantasy that I'd be a really fabulous father. Whether I would be or not, I don't know. I don't have the urge to procreate — whether it's an urge or whatever it is — and to a certain extent I've put it out of mind. And I'd like to leave it there.

L: But you still think about the people around you. You mentioned Gary. You think about what this might actually do in their lives, and how it might change them, in ways they don't know?

S: I'm interested in observing, rather than worrying, because other people think differently. I've seen the opposite situation of a gay man donating sperm to a straight woman, with him thinking that he wouldn't be terribly involved. It turned out that he was in fact incredibly attached to the child. Now he's got bored with the child and, in a funny way, it's the re-creation of that same heterosexual role-playing, but in this case it's a gay man. So you can't predict. It's very individual-specific.

L: What you were saying before about children wanting to know, I'd have to take issue with that, because while my children do, others I know have been brought up with the idea that "Daddy was a sperm-donor, and he's in England now," or "We don't know who he is, but we could probably find out if you really wanted to know," and the kids basically couldn't give a damn. They're very happy with their two mums.

S: How old are they?

L: About fourteen, ten and seven.

S: I want to know who my real parents were.

L: You don't know?

S: Of course I do! But I suspect the real ones were incredibly rich. [Laughter]

L: Our own parents are disturbingly and boringly our own!

S: Yes.

L: I always wanted to be adopted, too. I could never imagine why anybody would ever drop me down in this totally unreal suburban household. Obviously, for some of the children of lesbian families, it's a good thing that some gay donors want to be involved to some

140

extent, whether as uncles or fathers. From the beginning my feelings were, "Not heavily involved, thanks, because that could be a problem." The level of involvement now is fine; he's there, we know we can ring him up when we want to, we can turn him on and off. [Laughter]

S: Get money ... [Laughter]

L: No, they're totally unmaterialistic, they don't think that.

S: Oh, they will!

L: No, it's more the emotional stuff. Maybe they'll think that later. They like to know that there is a father out there, but I don't think that's true for all children.

S: You can't predict ... There's Liz Fell looking at us!

Liz: This party's full of rooms of people being interviewed. I mean, Bruce is in there, you're here, and it's a party! Is this the chapter he never wrote?

L: You're not the person who warned him off, are you?

Liz: No, no, I tried to encourage him.

S: Liz had a great title for it, which is — go on —

Liz: Well, I was thinking of Peter, Paul and Mary: "Where have all the sperm gone?"

S: "Long time passing."

L: Sasha, do the legal aspects of gay donoring concern you at all? Do you foresee a future litigation boom, when donored children start going their biological fathers for the family silver?

S: They might, but I'm the wrong person to talk to about legalities, because I think the law's bunk, absolute bunk.

L: Do you think that might be a problem, though, further down the track?

S: If it comes to that, I think they should be generous. [Laughter] I've always said that one's relationship with one's parents should be purely financial. They should offer before it becomes litigated.

L: Are you concerned that something called the 'gay identity' or gay lifestyle, if there is such a thing, will be compromised by some men's new concern with, and sense of responsibility for, their donored children?

S: I have to 'moo' to that question. All those things like 'gay identity' and 'gay lifestyle' — they change, year by year, decade by decade.

L: So why shouldn't a gay man be a parent, be a sperm donor, an uncle, be whatever he wants to be? As long as he's considered the options, and considered what he's doing?

S: There are other people involved, and the other people have to be considered as well. George Finey, he's dead now, he was a cartoonist and a really good painter. I interviewed him years ago, he was about 75 at that stage. He said to me, "There's one question I can't answer: Why is there life?" And I thought, "Oh, yeah, George." But it struck a chord in me, because I've sometimes thought — and this is complete fantasy — if ever I had the choice, I would probably not have chosen to be born. That's partly because I think that consciousness gives you a false state of being. There is an assumption that consciousness will continue, an identity will continue. And the lie, of course, is that it doesn't, it stops. I'm not sure that on a funny sort of metaphysical level that isn't part of my makeup of not having children.

L: That you think it's all going to finish anyway?

S: No, I don't mind if other people decide to do it. I feel that life is terrific, but it's also, underneath it all, a bit of a cheat.

L: But some people might want to perpetuate themselves like this.

S: I don't think they are perpetuating themselves. I fear they are bringing another person into the world who might suffer these same problems.

L: You're not referring to 'the gay gene', are you?

S: No, no, no, no. The problems of life.

L: The burdens of consciousness itself?

S: Yes. And I don't even mean things like starvation, or extreme unhappiness, or schizophrenia, or being disabled, or anything like that. I just mean day to day living, and the consciousness of death.

L: How many people, though, would choose not to be? If you don't know what consciousness is, how can you make a choice?

S: It's completely hypothetical, but that's one of the little philosophical things that I've been playing with, in thinking about this question.

L: In a sense you don't feel you have the right to bring into being other consciousnesses?

S: No. But once they're here, I'm glad they're here! [Laughter] It's that decision, it's that line you cross. I feel a bit incapable of crossing that line.

L: It seems to imply a tremendous commitment to life.

S: It also implies a certain amount of selfishness. In both respects — a selfishness of thinking that this person who's going to be born will want to be born, and a selfishness of wanting to reproduce. And the selfishness, also, of not wanting to reproduce. I don't like having pets, for example, because I don't particularly wish to be responsible. I'm not sure that I could completely, truthfully, say that if I donated sperm I would be able to abrogate that responsibility.

L: Is this responsibility any *more* for gay people, than it is for straight people? They could equally be accused of selfishness — for example, those people who have ten children.

142

S: I can't answer that, because it's not me. On this level I can only talk about me, really. Even though I listen to Geraldine Doogue religiously, I don't really have enough first-hand experience. I just don't know. I went back through that bottom line, and that bottom line meant "Did I want to be here?" and the answer was, "Probably not."

L: So why don't you top yourself?

S: Now that I'm here I don't want to go. [Laughter]

L: That's the logical extension of that sort of argument.

S: Oh no. The logical extension is to stay on as long as ~~~ ~~~.

L: Do you think gay donoring is an ego trip?

S: Not that I've observed.

L: Do you think it might give gay men an opportunity to prove their maleness in a very visible way to the straight world? Some gay men are looking at those children and saying, "It's really interesting seeing my genes in those kids, and how they all look alike ..."

S: How they all look like one particular sperm donor?

L: Not mentioning any names! [Laughter] ... and I've thought, "Hey, the woman is half the gene input here."

S: Yeah, that's right. "And my parents were a quarter input" — you can go back through history, so it's not just 'my genes'.

L: I wonder just how wide-spread this phenomenon would be?

S: I think that the phenomenon of feeling that you possess children is incredibly wide-spread. I had some friends over and one of the kids was climbing over the couch. His mother came over and slapped him and I thought, "Not in my house, you don't!" I do start from the premise that people are perfect. All people, and you've just got to find the entrance into their philosophical world which is unique, and discover that perfection. I don't censure, or I try not to. So, is it an ego-trip? Gay men are still men. In our patriarchal society, which hasn't improved terribly much, they still have, stuck to the back of their minds, all that training that they had when they weren't gay, when they were boys training to be men.

L: They've still got a patriarchal mind-set, even radicals, even those who are politically aware?

S: I don't think people change very much. The altering part is when you realise what you're about to do and you can stop it. I was brought up in a Russian household in a Russian community in Melbourne, as an anti-Semite. And I will be an anti-Semite until the day I die, but I'm aware of it and I know how to stop it. I know when the illogicality suddenly creeps into my mind. The argument goes on in my head, it doesn't go on in public. A lot of gay men still haven't come to grips with their masculinity in a patriarchal society.

L: What about the men who don't succeed in fathering children? How will it affect their self-esteem?

S: They're total failures! You see it all the time on television, those unhappy straight couples who will go to any extent to have this little ball of fluff that will turn around in twenty years time and hate them! And you kind of think, why can't you —

L: Get a dog or a cat?

S: Or enjoy other people's company. What always strikes me about those couples is that they never seem to have very many friends. So they put themselves into this narrowing circle where there's only one thing that will give them total satisfaction in life. Germaine Greer is a very interesting example in that respect. She was desperate to have a child, and she has lived through adopting various other people's children. Whether that's successful or not, that's another question.

L: That's a healthier alternative, isn't it?

S: I find it a bit strange when men talk about how they will have an uncle role. I always feel that an uncle role has an unconscious sexual element to it. Why can't they just be a friend or, "I am Bill and you are John"?

L: There's this compulsion towards using familial language, as a way of making it respectable.

S: You'll notice that I hardly ever talk about girl-children. I would be totally at sea bringing up a girl.

L: Because you haven't experienced being a girl? But then, straight fathers haven't either.

S: The early years of a girl are a total mystery to me.

L: I feel like that about boys. I had to have my eldest son circumcised, and I didn't have any concept about what an uncircumcised male was all about. I felt ill-equipped to deal with it.

S: What we're dealing with here is lack of knowledge. As probably the only gay person in my biological family's extended nuclear family, I have a different role now, in regard to children, because my mother comes to me for advice about my brother's kids. They suddenly got very worried about the middle girl because she was going along to male members of the family and sitting down and rubbing against their crutches, while sitting on their knees. I said, "Just leave her alone because she'll either resolve it herself or become embarrassed, but don't talk to her about it. Don't make it an issue." Knowing my family the talk would be hysterical — "We have to take her to a doctor" and all of that stuff. I said, "Just treat it as perfectly natural and it will stop." At which point my mother said, "Yes, I remember when you were a child you used to play with your dick a lot," and I thought, "I can't even remember that, thank you for this piece of information!" [Laughter] Comforting. Look, I admire people who bring up children, because I think it's a job and a half, if not more. I've said this over and over again, I don't think our society treats parents well enough. I think every parent should be given a dishwasher, a washing-machine and a dryer as soon as their child is born — make machines work. That takes away part of the drudgery. I wouldn't like to be responsible for bringing a child into the world that I couldn't look after to the best advantage of that society. Margaret Fink says you've got to choose a father who has good skin, great teeth, and lots of money. They were her three criteria.

L: Might there be a suggestion of a revenge motive in some donors' attitudes? That in some way not clearly understood, a la the gay gene theory, gayness will be perpetuated in the Australian population?

S: I think that's just perverse politics. I wouldn't be surprised if some people did take this seriously. I think there are millions of reasons why people turn gay. One of the things that's not accepted at the moment is that some people *choose.*

L: A lot of gays themselves won't accept that. See, see, it's all in the genes, we told you!

S: I know, and I just don't take that on board. The best example of that is people who over the course of a lifetime change their sexuality. Backwards and forwards, and celibate, sometimes. I have met a few people who are genuinely bisexual.

L: What most people mean by it is that they flip between one sex and the other.

S: Look, we were created by heterosexual parents, largely. On the question of donoring, I don't really have a political position. I don't know that I want to cope with the chore.

L: Why should you? — there's no compulsion.

S: I have this fantasy that I will be the uncle that my brother's children will run away to when they need to escape. But I'll be 67 before they've got a chance to run away, and why would they want to run away to me? I've had a bit of that experience with my step-sister's daughter, where she did actually run away to me, with her boyfriend, and they had a fabulous time. They stayed with me for about five days — they just went into a room and fucked. And I thought, why aren't you going out and seeing the Opera House, why don't you go for a walk? That's all they wanted to do.

My function was to say, "Hi, there's food in the fridge," when they emerged! I'm scared that there might be a back-lash, and the next generation won't have the slight number of open people to turn to that they have now. I'm very interested that, going to parties, I find myself talking to boys about 14 or 15. They actually make a beeline for me. I'm very confused about that. Part of it is that boys' sexuality is very very hidden, in the way that girls' sexuality isn't.

L: What is it that you perceive they want — just to talk?

S: Sometimes it's just to sit. Sit and watch. To see what someone you are interested in is all about, and what they're doing, and how the world relates to them. What was your first question again?

L: "You haven't given generously in these years of the lesbian baby-boom. Why not?"

S: Well, no one's ever really asked me, but then I think I've put out enough signals to say, "I don't think it's a wise thing to ask me." And my teeth aren't all that good.

Biographies and Acknowledgements
(In published order)

Louise Wakeling is a Sydney writer and parent who has co-edited and co-authored many books, including *Words from the same heart* (Hale & Iremonger, 1988) and *Rattling the Orthodoxies: a life of Ada Cambridge* (Penguin, 1991). *A Parachute of Blue,* a national poetry anthology co-edited with Judith Beveridge and Jill Jones, was launched in January 1995. Her first novel, *Saturn Return,* was published in 1990. She is currently writing a historical novel for her PhD at UNSW. A version of *Beyond Blood* appeared in *Famous Reporter,* December 1994.

Margaret Bradstock is a Sydney writer, reviewer, editor and academic. She is co-editor (with Louise Wakeling) of *Edge City on Two Different Plans* (inVersions), *Words from the Same Heart* (Hale & Iremonger), Ada Cambridge's *Thirty Years in Australia* (UNSW Press); and co-author of *small rebellions* (Wentworth) and *Rattling the Orthodoxies: a life of Ada Cambridge* (Penguin, 1991). Most recently she is author of a collection of poetry *Flight of Koalas* (BlackWattle), and is currently publishing feminist detective stories with Artemis.

Susan Harben is a mother, a feminist, a former President of Sydney Gay & Lesbian Mardi Gras, and the new ALP candidate for the state electorate of Bligh.

Cameron Sharp is currently an 'Uncty' in absentia from Wollongong's fair shores, visiting his extended family and many new arrivals since last in the northern hemisphere. On study leave he is touring, singing, free-lancing as a writer, washing dishes, and editing cable TV promos. He is 33, and still has to resolve his nomadic tendencies.

Sue Ogle was born in 1948 on the Harbour Bridge. Sue seems compelled to live in Sydney despite sixteen years away and daily plotting to escape to the South Coast. From her father, who completed an MA at 72, and her mother, who consults encyclopaedias and dictionaries regularly, she has acquired a habit for literature. She reads medical literature for her career as a doctor, and women's literature as an obsession. She feels grateful to her therapist for never really sorting her out. She has always written poetry and would die a happy woman if she could write one line of fiction with as much poetry and meaning as Toni Morrison. Bliss is surfing at Seven Mile Beach with Ben and Annie.

Annie Holstock grew up in Melbourne and still misses a proper winter. She trained and worked as a social worker and moved to Sydney late in life. Descended from a theatrical family she loves make up, dress ups, mess, glitter and music; perfect prerequisites for being a mother. Looking after Ben has given her the freedom to be creative, and she spends her time decorating boxes, making paper and handmade cards. She has never been happier.

Cliff Connors was born in Brisbane in 1949, into a Catholic family. He trained for missionary priesthood in Sydney between 1968-70 and left the Catholic Church in 1975 over its homophobia. He entered ministry in the Metropolitan Community Church in 1977, and became Dean of Australian Samaritan Education (the MCCs Theological College in Australia and NZ) in 1985. Cliff founded the MCC Good Shepherd in 1986 and has been pastoring there since then. Graduated as Master of Theology (Honours) from Sydney University in 1990 and was awarded Honorary Masters of Ministries by Australian Samaritan Education in 1992. Fourteen years in relationship with Stewart, his life partner.

Lea Crisante grew up in South-East Queensland, in a small farming district with a significant Italian community of which her family (who migrated to Australia in the early 1920s) formed part. She was one of the first women of her generation to attend university where she studied psychology. For the past fifteen years, much of her work as a therapist has been in working class and multicultural contexts in the inner and western Sydney. Currently, she is involved in a post-graduate training program for Relationship Counsellors. She teaches about diversity related to gender, sexual orientation, ethnicity, and class in order to enable therapists to work effectively and ethically with couples.

Miranda Kuijpers is originally from the Netherlands and migrated with her family to Australia in 1980. She is in a long-term relationship, raising a very charismatic, strong-willed seven year-old girl, Jordan. She recently joined the Gay and Lesbian Rights Lobby's committee, and has been involved in quite a number of 'family' issues, like donor insemination and unequal access to services for lesbians.

Belinda Vlotman is originally from South Africa, migrating to Australia in 1979 with her family. She met Miranda in 1989, and became involved in a relationship with her in 1990, when Jordan was two-and-a-half years old. At first it was difficult but now she wouldn't have it any other way. Her wish is that there was more written material available to give guidance to lesbians and gay men on 'How to parent'.

Rowan Savage is fourteen years old and hopes to be a writer. *Sick of hiding* received a 'Highly Commended' award in the *Sydney Morning Herald* Young Writers Competition, 1994.

Maeve Marsden is eleven years old; she lives with her two mums, her brother, her sister and her pets. She has never had any of her stories published but has always enjoyed story writing. She has had both good and bad things happen because of her parents, and has always taken their side.

Jay Walker is ten years old, and going on to an OC School (year five) in 1995. He is interested in acting and drama, swims competitively, is easily influenced by other children and reads a great deal. He hopes to be a writer, actor and computer programmer.

Julie Beauchamp qualified as an Occupational Therapist in 1976, and counselling patients and their families was always a large part of working in acute physical, community and psychiatric settings. In 1987 she completed training at Bouverie Family Therapy Centre (Melbourne). Worked at Prince Henry Hospital (Sydney) and then full-time with Relationships Australia (NSW) from 1988 including two years at the Adolescent Family Therapy and Mediation Service. Currently holds the position of senior counsellor and is a trainer in the Clinical Family Therapy Course.

Kerry Sawtell grew up in the western suburbs of Sydney; left school at 17 years old and travelled around a bit. At 23 she started studying law at night and graduated in 1988. She now lives in a rural town close to Sydney and is a practising lawyer. In between all that Kerry married, bore two children, divorced, came out as a lesbian; and now she's 37, sharing life with her partner and their friends, two children and their friends, three dogs and five cats. She's coped with all except the five cats.

Marilyn Mitchell is a part time TAFE teacher of adult literacy and ESOL to persons with a psychiatric disability. Marilyn herself has suffered from a schizo-affective disorder for fifteen years. She has three children (whose father is Chinese) and a female cat, Terry. She enjoys poetry, art architecture, walking and taking trips to restful places. Marilyn is currently completing Honours in Women's Studies at the University of Sydney.

Paul van Reyk is a gay writer, father, activist and sometime drag queen who looks forward to the day he has to fight his kids for the heels and frocks. *Donor Dads* has previously been published in *Capital Q*.

Gary Dunne edited *Fruit, a new anthology of contemporary gay writing(1993)* and *Travelling on Love in a Time of Uncertainty (1990)*, co-edited *Edge City on Two Different Plans(1983)*, and was fiction editor for *Burn* magazine. He's published three works of his own fiction, the most recent being *Shadows on the Dance Floor*. He lives in Sydney and his goal is to one day be a journalist. A version of *Happy little vegemites* was previously published in *Burn*.

Stephen Dunne recently discovered he can get a $5,000 fine and/or three years for this story. He would also like to correct the horrendous typo in his biography in *Fruit* — his computer is called 'Anouk', after Anouk Aimee, and not 'Drunk' as BlackWattle previously and evilly stated.

Pearlie MacNeill returned to Australia in April '94, after living in England for the past thirteen years. In Sydney during 1979 she and Marie McShea set up Womenwrite, a business venture concerned with publishing and bookselling. When that failed in 1981 she left for England and worked as a creative writing tutor there. She has published various titles, including a how-to book on writing — *Because You Want to Write* (Allen & Unwin, 1993) and an anthology of articles by Bosnian refugees.

Cathy Brooker grew up in Ryde and moved to the inner city about seven years ago. She has worked in the superannuation industry for the past five years, and now works in the area of assessment of medical retirement claims. Her main interests are travel, singing and renovating the 100 year old terrace house she shares with her husband. They are expecting their first child in March 1995.

Michael Bradstock grew up in Sydney's north-western suburbs, and is a computer network consultant. Interests include pool, outdoor cricket, indoor cricket, motorcycles and house renovation.

Stephanie Bradstock is a doctor living in Leichhardt with her male partner. She enjoys travel, writing and other art forms, and is trying to find time in her life to return to creativity. Currently raising a boxer named Ruby.

Teresa Savage is a Sydney writer currently enrolled in the MA writing program at the University of Technology. She has had many short stories, reviews and critical works published in Australia over the past seven years, and is currently working on a collection of pieces about contemporary lesbian experience. She lives with her partner and their three children.

Janet Peters currently lives with her partner and their two daughters in Chiang Mai, Northern Thailand. They have been there for a year and a half and will return home to Australia (Leichhardt!) in another year's time.

Sasha Soldatow lives in Bondi and is 47. He often prefers children to their parents.

MARGARET BRADSTOCK
FLIGHT OF KOALAS
contemporary poetry
ISBN 1 875243 10 0 — 67pg — RRP $9.95

This is a book about journeys, especially the journeys women make today — with all the baggage of desire, the need for knowledge, love and freedom. The poems take flight to various places: Europe, South-East Asia, the 500 bus route in Sydney, the Blue Mountains, and finally an impressive sequence about travelling in China. They explore the relationships between mother and daughter, the tragedy of AIDS, the difficult paths of feminism, the births and deaths of ordinary people.

'terse, immediate and keenly observant' —JUDITH BEVERIDGE. 'thoughtful, provocative, observant' —AUST BOOK REVIEW. 'Strong poems, fine perceptions' —JUDITH RODRIGUEZ

GARY DUNNE
SHADOWS ON THE DANCE FLOOR
contemporary gay fiction
ISBN 1 875243 11 9 — 96 pg — RRP $11.95

"Where there's hair, there's hope," states Mr Pointy Head, inner-city survivor, shoplifter and owner of three milk crates of second hand mens' underpants. Back in 1985 he and his ex-boyfriend Grace went for HIV blood tests together. It's now 1991 and, for the first time their different results really begin to matter. Nothing that Gary Dunne has previously written will prepare you for the hilarious yet poignant intensity of Shadows On The Dance Floor. It's an insider's story of a community where illness and death are common aspects of day to day living. With its dry wit and humour this novel powerfully captures an Australian response to AIDS.

'Regrettably familiar territory with sincerity, simplicity and devilish lashings of humour' —ROBERT JOHNSTON, CAMPAIGN. 'Brittle and extremely camp, a tough comic novel' —AUSTRALIAN BOOK REVIEW. 'Undoubted skill in the way the colloquial dryness and the quick trot of the narrative guide the book to a confronting yet witty resilience' —THE AUSTRALIAN. 'For once I agree with the blurb' —CAMPION DECENT, SYDNEY STAR OBSERVER. 'Says a great deal about contemporary Australia and has heart' —DIANA SIMMONDS, THE BULLETIN. 'This is a splendid book ... the kind of testament of which we who are of that generation can be proud.' —PAUL VAN REYK, TALKABOUT

Editors - Roberta Snow - Jill Taylor
FALLING FOR GRACE
an anthology of australian lesbian fiction
ISBN 1 875243 12 7 — 147 pg — RRP $14.95

Drawing together diverse lesbian lives, from feminist to gay lib, from coalitionist to queer, from suburban to chic — for the first time a wide ranging collection of Australian lesbian prose in one volume. 'Why is it imperative that you read this book? There are so many reasons. This lively volume rips back the veil of secrecy and silence … Stories of the 'dangerous tenderness' one woman can feel for another as she looks at 'softly tanned shoulders cut by the line of a pale blue singlet'. Stories of the inchoate longing that troubles and stirs the core of so many female friendships, as women instinctively reach for each other within the very shadow of husbands and convention. Stories of 'stray lust' at an office party and of violent rage at the brutal prejudice, often whispered in ignorance, that lacerates the heart. Their sexual love for each other is confidently expressed, whether in the 'carpet-lined smoke boxes' of an urban bar, or in the very bosom of the family at an Aussie wedding, where the bridesmaid has her eye on the bride.'

Dr Mary Hartman from the Foreword

'A treasure-trove of an anthology' —ROBYN STONE, LESBIANS ON THE LOOSE. 'Exhilarating confusion of style and contributors and subject matter, the mix is eclectic and balanced' —JENNY PAUSACKER, OUTRAGE. 'A shining display of lesbian literary talent' —SHÂN SHORT, BURN. 'Refreshing … reminds us that the diversity of real life is a fine thing' — TINA MUNCASTER, AUSTRALIAN BOOK REVIEW. 'Robust moments of comedy … lovely mix of eroticism and eccentricity' —CAMPAIGN. 'There's something for everyone here and lots, lots more.' GRACE DANGER, SYDNEY STAR OBSERVER.

BlackWattle Press Books

feisty, fast and fabulous fiction; perfect, pertinent poetry

Available from good family bookshops everywhere, just ask or write to PO Box 4, Leichhardt NSW 2040 (incl $2 postage)